REPORT OF EVIDENCE IN THE DEMOCRATS' IMPEACHMENT INQUIRY IN THE HOUSE OF REPRESENTATIVES

Republican Staff Report Prepared For

Devin Nunes
Ranking Member
Permanent Select Committee on Intelligence

Jim Jordan
Ranking Member
Committee on Oversight and Reform

Michael T. McCaul
Ranking Member
Committee on Foreign Affairs

December 2, 2019

EXECUTIVE SUMMARY

On November 8, 2016, nearly 63 million Americans from around the country chose Donald J. Trump to be the 45th President of the United States. Now, less than a year before the next presidential election, 231 House Democrats in Washington, D.C., are trying to undo the will of the American people.[*] As one Democrat admitted, the pursuit of this extreme course of action is because they want to stop President Trump's re-election.[†]

Democrats in the House of Representatives have been working to impeach President Trump since his election. Democrats introduced four separate resolutions in 2017 and 2018 seeking to impeach President Trump.[‡] In January 2019, on their first day in power, House Democrats again introduced articles of impeachment.[§] That same day, a newly elected Congresswoman promised to an audience of her supporters, "we're going to go in there and we're going to impeach the [expletive deleted]."[**] Her comments are not isolated. Speaker Nancy Pelosi called President Trump "an impostor" and said it is "dangerous" to allow American voters to evaluate his performance in 2020.[††]

The Democrats' impeachment inquiry is not the organic outgrowth of serious misconduct; it is an orchestrated campaign to upend our political system. The Democrats are trying to impeach a duly elected President based on the accusations and assumptions of unelected bureaucrats who disagreed with President Trump's policy initiatives and processes. They are trying to impeach President Trump because some unelected bureaucrats were discomforted by an elected President's telephone call with Ukrainian President Volodymyr Zelensky. They are trying to impeach President Trump because some unelected bureaucrats chafed at an elected President's "outside the beltway" approach to diplomacy.

The sum and substance of the Democrats' case for impeachment is that President Trump abused his authority to pressure Ukraine to investigate former Vice President Joe Biden, President Trump's potential political rival, for President Trump's benefit in the 2020 election. Democrats say this pressure campaign encompassed leveraging a White House meeting and the release of U.S. security assistance to force the Ukrainian President to succumb to President Trump's political wishes. Democrats say that Mayor Rudy Giuliani, the President's personal attorney, and a "shadow" group of U.S. officials conspired to benefit the President politically.

The evidence presented does not prove any of these Democrat allegations, and none of the Democrats' witnesses testified to having evidence of bribery, extortion, or any high crime or misdemeanor.

---

[*] H. Res. 660, 116th Cong. (2019) (Roll call vote 604).

[†] *Weekends with Alex Witt* (MSNBC television broadcast May 5 2019) (interview with Rep. Al Green).

[‡] H., Res. 705, 115th Cong. (2018); H. Res. 646, 115th Cong. (2017); H. Res. 621, 115th Cong. (2017); H. Res. 438, 115th Cong. (2017).

[§] H. Res. 13, 116th Cong. (2019).

[**] Amy B. Wong, *Rep. Rashida Tlaib profanely promised to impeach Trump. She's not sorry.*, Wash. Post, Jan. 4, 2019.

[††] Emily Tillett, *Nancy Pelosi says Trump's attacks on witnesses "very significant" to impeachment probe*, CBS News, Nov. 15, 2019; Dear Colleague Letter from Speaker Nancy Pelosi (Nov. 18, 2019).

The evidence does not support the accusation that President Trump pressured President Zelensky to initiate investigations for the purpose of benefiting the President in the 2020 election. The evidence does not support the accusation that President Trump covered up the summary of his phone conversation with President Zelensky. The evidence does not support the accusation that President Trump obstructed the Democrats' impeachment inquiry.

At the heart of the matter, the impeachment inquiry involves the actions of only two people: President Trump and President Zelensky. The summary of their July 25, 2019, telephone conversation shows no *quid pro quo* or indication of conditionality, threats, or pressure—much less evidence of bribery or extortion. The summary reflects laughter, pleasantries, and cordiality. President Zelensky has said publicly and repeatedly that he felt no pressure. President Trump has said publicly and repeatedly that he exerted no pressure.

Even examining evidence beyond the presidential phone call shows no *quid pro quo*, bribery, extortion, or abuse of power. The evidence shows that President Trump holds a deep-seated, genuine, and reasonable skepticism of Ukraine due to its history of pervasive corruption. The President has also been vocal about his skepticism of U.S. foreign aid and the need for European allies to shoulder more of the financial burden for regional defense. Senior Ukrainian officials under former President Petro Poroshenko publicly attacked then-candidate Trump during the 2016 campaign—including some senior Ukrainian officials who remained in their positions after President Zelensky's term began. All of these factors bear on the President's state of mind and help to explain the President's actions toward Ukraine and President Zelensky.

Understood in this proper context, the President's initial hesitation to meet with President Zelensky or to provide U.S. taxpayer-funded security assistance to Ukraine without thoughtful review is entirely prudent. Ultimately, President Zelensky took decisive action demonstrating his commitment to promoting reform, combatting corruption, and replacing Poroshenko-era holdovers with new leadership in his Administration. President Trump then released security assistance to Ukraine and met with President Zelensky in September 2019—all without Ukraine taking any action to investigate President Trump's political rival.

House Democrats allege that Ukraine felt pressure to bend to the President's political will, but the evidence shows a different reality. Ukraine felt good about its relationship with the United States in the early months of the Zelensky Administration, having had several high-level meetings with senior U.S. officials between July and September. Although U.S. security assistance was temporarily paused, the U.S. government did not convey the pause to the Ukrainians because U.S. officials believed the pause would get worked out and, if publicized, may be mischaracterized as a shift in U.S. policy towards Ukraine. U.S. officials said that the Ukrainian government in Kyiv never knew the aid was delayed until reading about it in the U.S. media. Ambassador Kurt Volker, the key American interlocutor trusted by the Ukrainian government, said the Ukrainians never raised concerns to him until after the pause became public in late August.

The Democrats' impeachment narrative ignores Ukraine's dramatic transformation in its fight against endemic corruption. President Trump was skeptical of Ukrainian corruption and his Administration sought proof that newly-elected President Zelensky was a true reformer. And after winning a parliamentary majority, the new Zelensky administration took rapid strides to crack down on corruption. Several high-level U.S. officials observed firsthand these anti-corruption achievements in Kyiv, and the security assistance was released soon afterward.

The Democrats' impeachment narrative also ignores President Trump's steadfast support for Ukraine in its war against Russian occupation. Several of the Democrats' witnesses described how President Trump's policies toward Ukraine to combat Russian aggression have been substantially stronger than those of President Obama—then under the stewardship of Vice President Biden. Where President Obama and Vice President Biden gave the Ukrainians night-vision goggles and blankets, the Trump Administration provided the Ukrainians with lethal defensive assistance, including Javelin anti-tank missiles.

The Democrats nonetheless tell a story of an illicit pressure campaign run by President Trump through his personal attorney, Mayor Giuliani, to coerce Ukraine to investigate the President's political rival by withholding a meeting and security assistance. There is, however, no direct, firsthand evidence of any such scheme. The Democrats are alleging guilt on the basis of hearsay, presumptions, and speculation—all of which are reflected in the anonymous whistleblower complaint that sparked this inquiry. The Democrats' narrative is so dependent on speculation that one Democrat publicly justified hearsay as "better" than direct evidence.‡‡ Where there are ambiguous facts, the Democrats interpret them in a light most unfavorable to the President. In the absence of real evidence, the Democrats appeal to emotion—evaluating how unelected bureaucrats *felt* about the events in question.

The fundamental disagreement apparent in the Democrats' impeachment inquiry is a difference of world views and a discomfort with President Trump's policy decisions. To the extent that some unelected bureaucrats believed President Trump had established an "irregular" foreign policy apparatus, it was because they were not a part of that apparatus. There is nothing illicit about three senior U.S. officials—each with official interests relating to Ukraine—shepherding the U.S.-Ukraine relationship and reporting their actions to State Department and NSC leadership. There is nothing inherently improper with Mayor Giuliani's involvement as well because the Ukrainians knew that he was a conduit to convince President Trump that President Zelensky was serious about reform.

There is also nothing wrong with asking serious questions about the presence of Vice President Biden's son, Hunter Biden, on the board of directors of Burisma, a corrupt Ukrainian company, or about Ukraine's attempts to influence the 2016 presidential election. Biden's Burisma has an international reputation as a corrupt company. As far back as 2015, the Obama State Department had concerns about Hunter Biden's role on Burisma's board. Ukrainian anti-corruption activists noted concerns as well. Publicly available—and irrefutable—evidence shows how senior Ukrainian government officials sought to influence the 2016 U.S. presidential election in opposition to President Trump's candidacy, and that some in the Ukrainian embassy in Washington worked with a Democrat operative to achieve that goal. While Democrats reflexively dismiss these truths as conspiracy theories, the facts are indisputable and bear heavily on the Democrats' impeachment inquiry.

---

‡‡ *"Impeachment Inquiry: Ambassador William B. Taylor and Mr. George Kent": Hearing before the H. Perm. Sel. Comm. on Intelligence*, 116th Cong. (2019) (statement of Rep. Mike Quigley).

* * *

In our system of government, power resides with the American people, who delegate executive power to the President through an election once every four years. Unelected officials and career bureaucrats assist in the execution of the laws. The unelected bureaucracy exists to serve the elected representatives of the American people. The Democrats' impeachment narrative flips our system on its head in service of their political ambitions.

The Democrats' impeachment inquiry, led by House Intelligence Committee Chairman Adam Schiff, is merely the outgrowth of their obsession with re-litigating the results of the 2016 presidential election. Despite their best efforts, the evidence gathered during the Democrats' partisan and one-sided impeachment inquiry does not support that President Trump pressured Ukraine to investigate his political rival to benefit the President in the 2020 presidential election. The evidence does not establish any impeachable offense.

But that is not for Democrats' want of trying.

For the first phase of the Democrats' impeachment inquiry, Chairman Schiff led the inquiry from his Capitol basement bunker, preventing transparency on the process and accountability for his actions. Because the fact-finding was unclassified, the closed-door process was purely for information control. This arrangement allowed Chairman Schiff—who had already publicly fabricated evidence and misled Americans about his interaction with the anonymous whistleblower—to selectively leak information to paint misleading public narratives, while simultaneously imposing a gag rule on Republican members. From his basement bunker, Chairman Schiff provided no due process protections for the President and he directed witnesses called by the Democrats not to answer Republican questions. Chairman Schiff also ignored Republican requests to secure the testimony of the anonymous whistleblower, despite promising earlier that the whistleblower would provide "unfiltered testimony."

When the Democrats emerged from the bunker for the public phase of their impeachment inquiry, Chairman Schiff continued to deny fundamental fairness and minority rights. Chairman Schiff interrupted Republican Members and directed witnesses not to answer Republican questions. Chairman Schiff refused to allow Republicans to exercise the limited procedural rights afforded to them. Chairman Schiff rejected witnesses identified by Republicans who would inject some semblance of fairness and objectivity. Chairman Schiff denied Republican subpoenas for testimony and documents, violating the Democrats' own rules to vote down these subpoenas with no notice to Republicans.

Speaker Pelosi, Chairman Schiff, and House Democrats seek to impeach President Trump—not because they have proof of a high crime or misdemeanor, but because they disagreed with the President's actions and his policies. But in our system of government, the President is accountable to the American people. The accountability to the American people comes at the ballot box, not in House Democrats' star chamber.

iv

FINDINGS

Democrats allege that President Trump pressured Ukraine to initiate investigations into his political rival, former Vice President Biden, for the purpose of benefiting the President in the 2020 U.S. presidential election. The evidence does not support the Democrats' allegations. Instead, the findings outlined below are based on the evidence presented and information available in the public realm.

- President Trump has a deep-seated, genuine, and reasonable skepticism of Ukraine due to its history of pervasive corruption.

- President Trump has a long-held skepticism of U.S. foreign assistance and believes that Europe should pay its fair share for mutual defense.

- President Trump's concerns about Hunter Biden's role on Burisma's board are valid. The Obama State Department noted concerns about Hunter Biden's relationship with Burisma in 2015 and 2016.

- There is indisputable evidence that senior Ukrainian government officials opposed President Trump's candidacy in the 2016 election and did so publicly. It has been publicly reported that a Democratic National Committee operative worked with Ukrainian officials, including the Ukrainian Embassy, to dig up dirt on then-candidate Trump.

- The evidence does not establish that President Trump pressured Ukraine to investigate Burisma Holdings, Vice President Joe Biden, Hunter Biden, or Ukrainian influence in the 2016 election for the purpose of benefiting him in the 2020 election.

- The evidence does not establish that President Trump withheld a meeting with President Zelensky for the purpose of pressuring Ukraine to investigate Burisma Holdings, Vice President Joe Biden, Hunter Biden, or Ukrainian influence in the 2016 election.

- The evidence does not support that President Trump withheld U.S. security assistance to Ukraine for the purpose of pressuring Ukraine to investigate Burisma Holdings, Vice President Joe Biden, Hunter Biden, or Ukrainian influence in the 2016 election.

- The evidence does not support that President Trump orchestrated a shadow foreign policy apparatus for the purpose of pressuring Ukraine to investigate Burisma Holdings, Vice President Joe Biden, Hunter Biden, or Ukrainian influence in the 2016 election.

- The evidence does not support that President Trump covered up the substance of his telephone conversation with President Zelensky by restricting access to the call summary.

- President Trump's assertion of longstanding claims of executive privilege is a legitimate response to an unfair, abusive, and partisan process, and does not constitute obstruction of a legitimate impeachment inquiry.

TABLE OF CONTENTS

TABLE OF NAMES

Christopher Anderson	Foreign Service Officer, U.S. Department of State
Michael Atkinson	Inspector General of the Intelligence Community (May 2018–present)
Arsen Avakov	Ukrainian Minister of Internal Affairs (February 2014–present)
Hunter Biden	Board Member, Burisma Holdings (April 2014–October 2019)
Joseph R. Biden	Vice President of the United States (January 2009–January 2017)
Robert Blair	Senior Advisor to the White House Chief of Staff (January 2019–present)
Andriy Bohdan	Head of Ukrainian Office of Presidential Administration (May 2019–present)
John Bolton	U.S. National Security Advisor (April 2018–September 2019)
T. Ulrich Brechbuhl	Counselor to the U.S. Secretary of State, U.S. Department of State (May 2018–present)
Alexandra Chalupa	Former contractor, Democratic National Committee
Valeriy Chaly	Ukrainian Ambassador to the United States (July 2015–July 2019)
Laura Cooper	Deputy Assistant Secretary of Defense for Russia, Ukraine, and Eurasia, U.S. Department of Defense
Catherine Croft	Foreign Service Officer, U.S. Department of State Director for European Affairs, National Security Council (July 2017–July 2018)
Oleksandr Danylyuk	Secretary of the Ukrainian National Security and Defense Council (May 2019–September 2019)
Michael Duffey	Associate Director for National Security Programs, U.S. Office of Management and Budget (May 2019–present)
John Eisenberg	Legal Advisor, National Security Council (2017–present)
Michael Ellis	Deputy Legal Advisor, National Security Council (March 2017–present)
Rudy Giuliani	Mayor of New York City (1994–2001) Personal Attorney to President Trump (April 2018–present)
Preston Wells Griffith	Associate Director for Natural Resources, Energy & Science, U.S. Office of Management and Budget (April 2018–present)
David Hale	Under Secretary of State for Political Affairs, U.S. Department of State (August 2018–present)
Fiona Hill	Senior Director for European and Russian Affairs, National Security Council (April 2017–July 2019)
David Holmes	Political Counselor, U.S. Embassy Kyiv§§ (August 2017–present)

---

§§ Consistent with the U.S. Board on Geographic Names, this report spells the Ukrainian capital as "Kyiv" throughout.

Keith Kellogg	National Security Advisor to the Vice President (April 2018–present)
George Kent	Deputy Assistant Secretary of State, Bureau of European and Eurasian Affairs, U.S. Department of State (September 2018–present)
Igor Kolomoisky	Co-owner, PrivatBank Co-owner, 1+1 Media Group
Charles Kupperman	U.S. Deputy National Security Advisor (January 2019–September 2019)
Serhiy Leshchenko	Ukrainian Member of Parliament (November 2014–July 2019)
Yuriy Lutsenko	Prosecutor General of Ukraine (May 2016–August 2019)
Joseph Maguire	Acting U.S. Director of National Intelligence (August 2019–present)
Brian McCormack	Associate Director for Natural Resources, Energy & Science, U.S. Office of Management and Budget (September 2018–present)
Michael McKinley	Senior Advisor to the U.S. Secretary of State, U.S. Department of State (November 2018–October 2019)
Tim Morrison	Senior Director for European and Russian Affairs, National Security Council (July 2019–November 2019)
Mick Mulvaney	Director of the U.S. Office of Management and Budget (February 2017–present) Acting Chief of Staff to the President (January 2019–present)
Nellie Ohr	Contractor, Fusion GPS
Mike Pence	Vice President of the United States (January 2017–present)
Rick Perry	U.S. Secretary of Energy (March 2017–present)
Mike Pompeo	U.S. Secretary of State (April 2018–present)
Petro Poroshenko	President of Ukraine (June 2014–May 2019)
Vadym Prystaiko	Minister of Foreign Affairs of Ukraine (August 2019–present)
Philip Reeker	Acting Assistant Secretary of State, Bureau of European and Eurasian Affairs, U.S. Department of State (March 2019–present)
Mark Sandy	Deputy Associate Director for National Security, U.S. Office of Management and Budget (December 2013–present)
Viktor Shokin	Prosecutor General of Ukraine (February 2015–March 2016)
Oksana Shulyar	Deputy Chief of Mission, Embassy of Ukraine to the U.S.
Gordon Sondland	U.S. Ambassador to the European Union (July 2018–present)
William Taylor	U.S. Ambassador to Ukraine (June 2006–May 2009) U.S. Chargé d'Affaires, *a.i.*, U.S. Embassy Kyiv (June 2019–present)
Andrii Telizhenko	Political officer, Embassy of Ukraine to the U.S.
Donald J. Trump	President of the United States (January 2017–present)

Alexander Vindman	Director for European Affairs, National Security Council (July 2018–present)
Kurt Volker	U.S. Special Representative for Ukraine Negotiations, U.S. Department of State (July 2017–September 2019)
Russell Vought	Acting Director, U.S. Office of Management and Budget
Kathryn Wheelbarger	Acting Assistant Secretary of Defense for International Affairs, U.S. Department of Defense (November 2018–present)
Jennifer Williams	Special Adviser for Europe and Russia, Office of the Vice President
Viktor Yanukovych	President of Ukraine (February 2010–February 2014)
Arseniy Yatsenyuk	Prime Minister of Ukraine (February 2014–April 2016)
Andrey Yermak	Adviser to President of Ukraine Volodymyr Zelensky
Marie Yovanovitch	U.S. Ambassador to Ukraine (August 2016–May 2019)
Volodymyr Zelensky***	President of Ukraine (May 2019–present)
Mykola Zlochevsky	Co-founder, Burisma Holdings (2002–present) Ukrainian Minister of Ecology and Natural Resources (July 2010–April 2012)

*** Although some sources use alternate spellings of the Ukrainian President's surname, this report uses the spelling "Zelensky" for consistency throughout.

I. The evidence does not establish that President Trump pressured the Ukrainian government to investigate his political rival for the purpose of benefiting him in the 2020 U.S. presidential election.

Democrats have alleged that President Trump exerted pressure on Ukrainian President Zelensky to force the Ukrainian government to manufacture "dirt" or otherwise investigate a potential Democrat candidate in the 2020 U.S. presidential election for President Trump's political benefit.[1] Democrats allege that President Trump sought to use the possibility of a White House meeting with President Zelensky and release of U.S. security assistance to Ukraine as leverage to force Ukraine to help the President politically. Democrats allege that President Trump orchestrated a "shadow" foreign policy apparatus that worked to accomplish the President's political goals.

The evidence obtained in the Democrats' impeachment inquiry, however, does not support these Democrat allegations. In fact, witnesses called by the Democrats denied having any awareness of criminal activity or an impeachable offense. Rep. John Ratcliffe asked Ambassador Bill Taylor and Deputy Assistant Secretary George Kent whether they were "assert[ing] there was an impeachable offense in [the July 25] call."[2] Neither said there was.[3] Rep. Chris Stewart asked Ambassador Marie Yovanovitch if she had any information about President Trump's involvement in criminal activity.[4] Ambassador Yovanovitch said no.[5] Rep. Ratcliffe asked National Security Council (NSC) staff member LTC Alexander Vindman and Office of the Vice President special adviser Jennifer Williams if they have labeled the President's conduct as "bribery."[6] Both said no.[7] Rep. Elise Stefanik asked Ambassador Kurt Volker, the U.S. special envoy for Ukraine negotiations, and Tim Morrison, the NSC senior director for Europe, whether they saw any bribery, extortion, or *quid pro quo*.[8] Both said no.[9]

Contrary to Democrat assertions, the evidence does not show that President Trump pressured President Zelensky to investigate his political rival during the July 25 phone call. The best evidence of the conversation—the call summary—shows no evidence of conditionality, threats, or pressure. President Zelensky and President Trump have both said there was no

[1] *"Whistleblower Disclosure": Hearing of the H. Perm. Sel. Comm. on Intelligence*, 116th Cong. (2019) (statement of Rep. Adam Schiff, Chairman); Rep. Adam Schiff (@RepAdamSchiff), Twitter (Oct. 12, 2019, 2:53 p.m.), https://twitter.com/repadamschiff/status/1183138629130035200; *Lieu accuses Trump of asking Ukraine to "manufacture dirt" on Biden*, The Hill, Sept. 25, 2019.

[2] *"Impeachment Inquiry: Ambassador William B. Taylor and Mr. George Kent": Hearing before the H. Perm. Sel. Comm. on Intelligence*, 116th Cong. (2019).

[3] *Id.*

[4] *"Impeachment Inquiry: Ambassador Marie Yovanovitch": Hearing before the H. Perm. Sel. Comm. on Intelligence*, 116th Cong. (2019).

[5] *Id.*

[6] *"Impeachment Inquiry: LTC Alexander Vindman and Ms. Jennifer Williams": Hearing before the H. Perm. Sel. Comm. on Intelligence*, 116th Cong. (2019). This report abbreviates military titles consistent with the U.S. Government Printing Office style manual. *See* U.S. Gov't Printing Off., Style Manual 227 (2016).

[7] *Id.*

[8] *"Impeachment Inquiry: Ambassador Kurt Volker and Mr. Timothy Morrison": Hearing before the H. Perm. Sel. Comm. on Intelligence*, 116th Cong. (2019).

[9] *Id.*

pressure, the initial read-out from the State Department and the Ukrainian government reflected no concerns, and the NSC leadership saw no illegality or impropriety with the call.

The evidence does not show that President Trump withheld a meeting with President Zelensky to pressure Ukraine to investigate his political rival. The evidence shows that President Trump has a long-standing, deep-seated skepticism of Ukraine due to its history of pervasive corruption. President Zelensky was a political newcomer with untested views on anti-corruption and a close association with a Ukrainian oligarch. Even so, President Trump agreed to invite President Zelensky to the White House, and in the interim, Ukrainian officials had several high-level meetings with U.S. officials. President Trump and President Zelensky met in September 2019 without Ukraine ever taking any action on investigating President Trump's political rival.

In addition, the evidence does not show that President Trump withheld U.S. security assistance to Ukraine to pressure Ukraine to investigate his political rival. The evidence shows that President Trump has a skepticism of U.S. taxpayer-funded foreign aid and believes Europe should carry more financial burden for its regional defense. Although U.S. security assistance was paused temporarily, Democrats' witnesses denied there being any direct link to investigations of the President's political rival. Both the Ukrainian government and President Trump separately denied any linkage. U.S. officials did not tell the Ukrainian officials about the delay because they thought it would get worked out. Ambassador Volker, a senior U.S. diplomat and primary interlocutor with senior Ukrainian government officials, testified that the Ukrainians did not raise concerns to him about a delay in aid until after the pause was made public in late August 2019. The U.S. security assistance to Ukraine was ultimately disbursed without Ukraine taking any action to investigate President Trump's political rival.

The evidence does not show that President Trump established a "shadow" foreign policy apparatus to pressure Ukraine to investigate his political rival. The President has broad Constitutional authority over U.S. foreign policy, and President Trump is likely suspicious of the national security apparatus due to continual leaks of sensitive information and the resistance within the federal bureaucracy. The three U.S. officials who Democrats accuse of conducting an "irregular" foreign policy channel had legitimate responsibilities for Ukraine policy. They kept the State Department and NSC aware of their actions. To the extent Mayor Giuliani was involved, he was in communication with these officials and the Ukrainians did not see him as speaking on behalf of the President.

Although Democrats reflexively criticize President Trump for promoting "conspiracy theories" about Hunter Biden's role on Burisma's board or Ukrainian attempts to influence the 2016 election, evidence suggests there are legitimate questions about both issues. The Democrats' witnesses testified that it would be appropriate for Ukraine to investigate allegations of corruption in Ukraine.

Finally, there are fundamental flaws with the anonymous whistleblower complaint that initiated the Democrats' impeachment inquiry. The complaint contained inaccurate and misleading information that prejudiced the public understanding of President Trump's conversation with President Zelensky. The whistleblower had no firsthand knowledge of the events in question and a bias against President Trump. The whistleblower communicated with

Chairman Schiff or his staff prior to submitting the whistleblower complaint to the Inspector General of the Intelligence Community. Several witnesses contradicted assertions made by the anonymous whistleblower. The whistleblower's complaint did not accurately reflect the tone and substance of the phone call, which is unsurprising given the whistleblower's reliance on secondhand information that had likely already been colored by biases of the original sources.

A. The evidence does not establish that President Trump pressured President Zelensky during the July 25 phone call to investigate the President's political rival for the purpose of benefiting him in the 2020 election.

On July 25, 2019, President Trump and President Zelensky spoke by telephone.[10] This conversation would later serve as the basis for the anonymous whistleblower complaint and the spark for the Democrats' impeachment inquiry. Contrary to allegations that President Trump pressured Ukraine to investigate a domestic political rival during this call,[11] the evidence shows that President Trump did not pressure President Zelensky to investigate his political rival.

The call summary and initial read-outs of the conversation reflect no indication of conditionality, coercion, or intimidation—elements that would have been present if President Trump had used his authority to pressure President Zelensky to investigate his political rival. Importantly, both President Zelensky and President Trump have said publicly there was no pressure or anything inappropriate about their conversation. The anonymous whistleblower complaint—which sparked the impeachment inquiry—contains sensational rhetoric about the July 25 phone conservation that has prejudged subsequent views of the call.

1. The call summary does not reflect any improper pressure or conditionality to pressure Ukraine to investigate President Trump's political rival.

The best evidence of the telephone conversation between President Trump and President Zelensky is the contemporaneous summary prepared by the White House Situation Room. The Democrats' witnesses described how National Security Council (NSC) policy staffers and White House Situation Room duty officers typically listen in on presidential conversations with foreign leaders to transcribe the contents of the conversation.[12] This process occurred for President Trump's July 25 phone call with President Zelensky.

---

[10] President Trump had spoken with then-President-elect Zelensky on April 21, 2019, to congratulate him on his election. *See* The White House, *Memorandum of Telephone Conversation* (Apr. 21, 2019). This conversation too contained no indication of pressure, intimidation or threats. *See id.*

[11] *See, e.g.*, Josh Dawsey et al., *How Trump and Giuliani pressured Ukraine to investigate the President's rivals*, Wash. Post, (Sept. 20, 2019).

[12] *See, e.g.*, Deposition of Dr. Fiona Hill, in Wash., D.C., at 297-300 (Oct. 14, 2019) [hereinafter "Hill deposition"]. Although some have alleged that the presence of ellipses in the call summary connotes missing text, witnesses testified that call summaries often use ellipses to denote unfinished thoughts and not to "read too much" into the use of ellipses. *See, e.g., id.* at 307. LTC Vindman testified in his closed-door deposition that any editing decisions or missing words were not done maliciously. *See* Deposition of LTC Alexander Vindman, in Wash., D.C., at 253 (Oct. 29, 2019) [hereinafter "Vindman deposition"]. In his public testimony, LTC Vindman explained that although the summary did not mention the word "Burisma," it was "not a significant omission." *Impeachment Inquiry: LTC Alexander Vindman and Ms. Jennifer Williams, supra* note 6. Morrison testified in his deposition that he believed

As transcribed, the call summary denotes laughter, pleasantries, and compliments exchanged between President Trump and President Zelensky. The summary does not evince any threats, coercion, intimidation, or indication of conditionality. Democrats even acknowledged that the call summary reflected no *quid pro quo*.[13] The summary bears absolutely no resemblance to House Intelligence Committee Chairman Adam Schiff's self-described "parody" interpretation of the call, which the Chairman performed at a public hearing on September 26.[14]

The summary of the July 25 phone call begins by President Trump congratulating President Zelensky on a "great victory," a "terrific job," and a "fantastic achievement."[15] President Zelensky reciprocated by complimenting President Trump, saying:

> Well, yes, to tell you the truth, we are trying to work hard because we wanted to drain the swamp here in our country. We brought in many, many new people. Not the old politicians, not the typical politicians, because we want to have a new format and a new type of government. You are a great teacher for us and in that.[16]

President Trump expressed his concern that European countries were not providing their fair share in terms of assistance to Ukraine[17]—a topic about which President Trump has been vocal.[18] President Zelensky responded that President Trump was "absolutely right" and that he had expressed concerns to German Chancellor Angela Merkel and French President Emmanuel Macron.[19] President Zelensky thanked President Trump for U.S. military support and said Ukraine was "almost ready to buy more Javelins from the United States for defense purposes."[20]

President Trump then transitioned to discuss the allegation that some Ukrainian officials sought to influence the 2016 U.S. presidential election. Although Democrats have seized on the President's phrasing—"I would like you to do us a favor though"[21]—to accuse the President of pressuring President Zelensky to target his 2020 political rival for his political benefit,[22] they omit the remainder of his sentence. The full sentence shows that President Trump was not asking President Zelensky to investigate his political rival, but rather asking him to assist in "get[ting] to

---

the call memorandum was an "accurate and complete" reflection of the substance of the call. Deposition of Timothy Morrison, in Wash., D.C., at 60 (Oct. 31, 2019) [hereinafter "Morrison deposition"].

[13] *See, e.g.*, *MSNBC Live with Craig Melvin* (MSNBC television broadcast Sept. 25, 2019) (interview with Rep. Ro Khanna) (saying evidence of a *quid pro quo* on the call summary is "irrelevant").

[14] *Whistleblower Disclosure, supra* note 1.

[15] The White House, *Memorandum of Telephone Conversation* 1 (July 25, 2019).

[16] *Id.* at 2.

[17] *Id.*

[18] *See infra* section I.C.2.

[19] *Memorandum of Telephone Conversation, supra* note 15, at 2.

[20] *Id.*

[21] *Id.* at 3.

[22] *See, e.g.*, *Whistleblower Disclosure, supra* note 1 (statement of Rep. Adam Schiff, Chairman).

the bottom" of potential Ukrainian involvement in the 2016 election.[23] This reading is supported by President Trump's subsequent reference to Special Counsel Robert Mueller, who had testified the day before about his findings,[24] and to Attorney General William Barr, who had initiated an official inquiry into the origins of the U.S. government's 2016 Russia investigation.[25]

President Zelensky did not express any concern that President Trump had raised the allegations about Ukrainian influence in the 2016 election. In fact, President Zelensky responded by reiterating his commitment to cooperation between Ukraine and the United States and mentioning that he had recalled the Ukrainian Ambassador to the United States, Valeriy Chaly.[26] Ambassador Chaly had authored an op-ed in *The Hill* during the height of the presidential campaign in 2016 criticizing a statement that President Trump had made by Crimea.[27] President Zelensky said he planned to surround himself with "the best and most experienced people" and pledged that "as the President of Ukraine that all the investigations will be done openly and candidly."[28] President Zelensky also raised former New York Mayor Rudy Giuliani, saying "we are hoping very much that Mr. Giuliani will be able to travel to Ukraine and we will meet once he comes to Ukraine."[29]

The call summary shows that the discussion then intertwined several different topics. In response to President Zelensky's statement about new personnel, President Trump and President Zelensky discussed the position of prosecutor general.[30] President Zelensky did not express any discomfort discussing the prosecutor general position. He said the new prosecutor general would be "100% my person, my candidate" and said the prosecutor would look into the matters raised by President Trump to "mak[e] sure to restore the honesty" of the investigation.[31] President Zelensky later said "we will be very serious about the case and will work on the investigation."[32]

In response to President Zelensky's reference to Mayor Giuliani, President Trump said Mayor Giuliani is "a highly respected man" who "very much knows what's happening and he is a very capable guy."[33] President Trump said that he would ask Mayor Giuliani to call President Zelensky, along with Attorney General Barr, to "get to the bottom of it."[34] President Zelensky did not express any concern about Mayor Giuliani's engagement—in fact, President Zelensky, not President Trump, first referenced Mayor Giuliani in the conversation.

---

[23] *Memorandum of Telephone Conversation*, *supra* note 15, at 3. The President's reference to "Crowdstrike" during the conversation refers to a cybersecurity firm that examined the Democratic National Committee server following intrusion by the Russian government in 2016.

[24] *"Oversight of the Report on the Investigation into Russian Interference in the 2016 Presidential Election: Former Special Counsel Robert S. Mueller, III"*: Hearing before the H. Comm. on the Judiciary, 116th Cong. (2019).

[25] *See, e.g.*, Adam Goldman et al., *Barr assigns U.S. Attorney in Connecticut to review origins of Russia inquiry*, N.Y. Times, May 13, 2019.

[26] *Memorandum of Telephone Conversation*, *supra* note 15, at 3.

[27] Valeriy Chaly, *Ukraine's ambassador: Trump's comments send wrong message to world*, The Hill, Aug. 4, 2016.

[28] *Memorandum of Telephone Conversation*, *supra* note 15, at 3.

[29] *Id.*

[30] *Id.* at 3-4.

[31] *Id.* at 4.

[32] *Id.* at 5.

[33] *Id.* at 3-4.

[34] *Id.* at 4.

President Trump then raised former U.S. Ambassador to Ukraine, Marie Yovanovitch, saying that she was "bad news" and "the people she was dealing with in the Ukraine were bad news."[35] President Zelensky did not express any hesitancy in discussing the ambassador. Contrary to Democrats' assertion that he felt obligated to agree with President Trump's assessment, President Zelensky stated his independent negative assessment of Ambassador Yovanovitch:

> Her attitude toward me was far from the best as she admired the previous President and she was on his side. She would not accept me as a new President well enough.[36]

President Trump also raised in passing—using the transition phrase "the other thing"—the topic of Vice President Joe Biden's son, Hunter Biden, referring to his position on the board of a Ukrainian energy company, Burisma, known for its corruption.[37] President Trump said "a lot of people want to find out about that so whatever you can do with the Attorney General would be great."[38] President Zelensky did not reply to President Trump's reference to the Bidens, and the two did not discuss the topic substantively.

The call concluded with President Zelensky raising energy cooperation between Ukraine and the United States and with President Trump reiterating his invitation for President Zelensky to visit the White House.[39]

Although some later expressed concern about the call, the call summary—the best evidence of the conversation—shows no indication of conflict, intimidation, or pressure. President Trump never conditioned a White House meeting on any action by President Zelensky. President Trump never mentioned U.S. security assistance to Ukraine. President Zelensky never verbalized any disagreement, hostility, or concern about any facet of the U.S.-Ukrainian relationship.

2. President Zelensky has publicly and repeatedly said he felt no pressure to investigate President Trump's political rival.

Since President Trump declassified and publicly released the content of his July 25 phone conversation with President Zelensky, President Zelensky and other senior Ukrainian officials have publicly and repeatedly asserted that President Zelensky felt no pressure to investigate President Trump's political rival. President Zelensky has variously asserted, "nobody pushed . . . me," "I was never pressured," and there was no "blackmail."

---

[35] *Id.*
[36] *Id.*
[37] *Id.*
[38] *Id.*
[39] *Id.* at 5.

6

On September 25, President Zelensky and President Trump met face-to-face for a bilateral meeting on the margins of the 74th United Nations (U.N.) General Assembly in New York. The presidents jointly participated in a media availability, during which President Zelensky asserted that he felt no pressure.[40] President Zelensky said then:

> Q. President Zelensky, have you felt any pressure from President Trump to investigate Joe Biden and Hunter Biden?
>
> A. I think you read everything. So I think you read text. I'm sorry, but I don't want to be involved to democratic, open elections — elections of USA. *No, you heard that we had, I think, good phone call. It was normal. We spoke about many things. And I — so I think, and you read it, that nobody pushed — pushed me.*[41]

President Zelensky again reiterated that he was not pressured to investigate President Trump's political rival during an interview with a Kyodo News, a Japanese media outlet, published on October 6. Kyodo News quoted President Zelensky as saying, "I was never pressured and there were no conditions being imposed" on a White House meeting or U.S. security assistance to Ukraine.[42] President Zelensky denied "reports by U.S. media that [President] Trump's requests were conditions" for a White House meeting or U.S. security assistance.[43]

On October 10, during an all-day media availability in Kyiv, President Zelensky again emphasized that he felt no pressure to investigate President Trump's political rival. President Zelensky said there was "no blackmail" during the conversation, explaining: "This is not corruption. It was just a call."[44]

In addition, on September 21—before President Trump had even declassified and released the call summary—Ukrainian Foreign Minister Vadym Prystaiko denied that President Trump had pressured President Zelensky to investigate President Trump's political rival.[45] Foreign Minister Prystaiko said:

> *I know what the conversation was about and I think there was no pressure.* There was talk, conversations are different, leaders have the right to discuss any problems that exist. This conversation was

---

[40] Press Release, The White House, Remarks by President Trump and President Zelensky of Ukraine Before Bilateral Meeting (Sept. 25, 2019), *available at* https://www.whitehouse.gov/briefings-statements/remarks-president-trump-president-zelensky-ukraine-bilateral-meeting-new-york-ny/.

[41] *Id.* (emphasis added).

[42] *Ukraine president denies being pushed by Trump to investigate Biden*, Kyodo News, Oct. 6, 2019.

[43] *Id.*

[44] *Ukraine's president says 'no blackmail' in Trump call*, BBC, Oct. 10, 2019.

[45] *"Trump did not pressure Zelenskyy, Ukraine is independent state" – Foreign Minister Prystaiko*, Hromadske, Sept. 21, 2019.

long, friendly, and it touched on a lot of questions, including those requiring serious answers.[46]

Similarly, Ambassador Bill Taylor explained that he had dinner with Oleksandr Danylyuk, then-Secretary of the National Security and Defense Council, the night of the phone conversation between President Trump and President Zelensky.[47] He explained that Danylyuk said that the Ukrainian government "seemed to think that the call went fine, the call went well. He wasn't disturbed by anything. He wasn't disturbed that he told us about the phone call."[48]

President Zelensky's repeated denials that President Trump pressured him to investigate domestic political rival—corroborated by Foreign Minister Prystaiko's similar denial—carry significant weight.

3. President Trump has publicly and repeatedly said he did not pressure President Zelensky to investigate his political rival.

Like President Zelensky, President Trump has repeatedly and publicly stated that he did not pressure President Zelensky to investigate his political rival. During the September 25 bilateral meeting with President Zelensky, President Trump said to the assembled members of the media: "There was no pressure. And you know there was—and, by the way, you know there was no pressure. All you have to do it see it, what went on the call."[49] When asked whether he wanted President Zelensky to "do more" to investigate Vice President Biden, President Trump responded: "No. I want him to do whatever he can. This was not his fault; he wasn't there. He's just been here recently. But whatever he can do in terms of corruption, because the corruption is massive."[50]

Despite the President's statements, some allege that an overheard conversation the day after President Trump's conversation with President Zelensky shows that the President sought to pressure President Zelensky. On July 26, following a meeting with President Zelensky, Ambassador Gordon Sondland, the U.S. Ambassador to the European Union, telephoned President Trump from Kyiv.[51] According to a subsequent account of David Holmes, a Political Counselor at U.S. Embassy Kyiv, Ambassador Sondland told the President that he was in Ukraine and stated President Zelensky "loves your ass."[52] Holmes recounted that President Trump asked Ambassador Sondland, "So he's going to do the investigation?"[53] Ambassador Sondland allegedly replied, "He's going to do it."[54]

---

[46] *Id.* (emphasis added).
[47] Deposition of Ambassador William B. Taylor, in Wash., D.C., at 80 (Oct. 22, 2019).
[48] *Id.*
[49] Remarks by President Trump and President Zelensky of Ukraine Before Bilateral Meeting, *supra* note 40.
[50] *Id.*
[51] Deposition of David Holmes, in Wash., D.C., at 23-25 (Nov. 15, 2019) [hereinafter "Holmes deposition"]. Ambassador Sondland did not mention this phone call in his deposition. *See generally* Deposition of Ambassador Gordon D. Sondland, in Wash., D.C. (Oct. 17, 2019) [hereinafter "Sondland deposition"].
[52] Holmes deposition, *supra* note 51, at 24
[53] *Id.*
[54] *Id.*

8

This conversation is not definitive evidence that President Trump pressured President Zelensky to investigate his political rival. First, according to Ambassador Sondland, it was not clear that President Trump meant an investigation into the Bidens. In his closed-door deposition, Ambassador Sondland testified that he only had "five or six" conversations with the President and did not mention this particular conversation.[55] In his public testimony, however, Ambassador Sondland suddenly recalled the conversation, saying that it "did not strike me as significant at the time" and that the primary purpose of the call was to discuss rapper A$AP Rocky, who was imprisoned in Sweden.[56] Ambassador Sondland testified that he has no recollection of discussing Vice President Biden or his son, Hunter Biden, with President Trump.[57]

Second, Holmes testified that although he disclosed Ambassador Sondland's conversation with the President to multiple friends on multiple occasions, he did not feel compelled to disclose it to the State Department or Congress until weeks into the impeachment inquiry.[58] Although Holmes testified that he told his boss, Ambassador Taylor, about the call on August 6 and received a "knowing" response, and that he referred to the call often in staff meetings, Ambassador Taylor testified publicly that he was "not aware of this information" at the time of his October 22 deposition, and that he only became aware of the Holmes account on November 8, 2019, two days after his hearing was publicly announced, at which point he referred it (for the first time) to the Legal Adviser for the Department of State.[59]

4. Read-outs of the phone call from both the State Department and the Ukrainian government did not reflect that President Trump pressured President Zelensky to investigate his political rival.

Immediately following the telephone conversation between President Trump and President Zelensky, senior U.S. and Ukrainian government officials provided read-outs of the conversation. According to witness testimony, none of these read-outs indicated that the conversation between the presidents was substantively concerning.

Ambassador Volker testified that he received informal read-outs of the call from both his State Department assistant and his high-level Ukrainian contacts.[60] These read-outs did not indicate any concern with the phone call. Ambassador Volker explained:

---

[55] Sondland deposition, *supra* note 51, at 56.

[56] *"Impeachment Inquiry: Ambassador Gordon Sondland": Hearing before the H. Perm. Sel. Comm. on Intelligence*, 116th Cong. (2019).

[57] *Id.*

[58] Holmes deposition, *supra* note 51, at 31, 158-62.

[59] *Id.* at 81-82, 121-22, 167; *see generally* Taylor deposition, *supra* note 47; *Impeachment Inquiry: Ambassador William B. Taylor and Mr. George Kent*, *supra* note 2.

[60] Transcribed interview of Ambassador Kurt Volker, in Wash., D.C., at 102-03 (Oct. 3, 2019) [hereinafter "Volker transcribed interview"]. Ambassador Volker's assistant at the time, Catherine Croft, testified that she only received a read-out of the phone call was based on what President Zelensky told Ambassador Volker, Ambassador Taylor, and Ambassador Sondland on July 26. Deposition of Catherine Croft, in Wash., D.C., at 16 (Oct. 30, 2019) [hereinafter "Croft deposition"].

A. I got an oral readout from the staffer who works for me in the State Department and our chargé, as well as from Andrey Yermak, who had been on the call in Ukraine himself.

Q. So you got two readouts?

A. Yeah.

Q. One from each side?

A. Correct.

Q. What was the top line message you got from the State Department?

A. Well, they were the same, actually, which is interesting. But the message was congratulations from the President to President Zelensky; President Zelensky reiterating that he is committed to fighting corruption and reform in the Ukraine; and President Trump reiterating an invitation for President Zelensky to visit him at the White House. That was it.[61]

In fact, in his public testimony, Ambassador Volker testified that President Zelensky was "very upbeat about the fact of the call."[62]

Ambassador Sondland received a summary of the phone call from his staff.[63] Ambassador Sondland testified that he was pleased to learn that it was a "good call."[64] George Kent, the Deputy Assistant Secretary of State covering Ukraine, testified that he received a read-out of the call from NSC staffer LTC Alexander Vindman.[65] According to Kent, although LTC Vindman said the "atmospherics" of the conversation was cooler and reserved, LTC Vindman did not mention Vice President Biden's name or anything relating to 2016.[66]

In addition, the Office of the President of Ukraine issued an official statement following the phone call.[67] The official statement also signaled no concern about the call or any indication of coercion, intimidation, or pressure from President Trump. The statement read in full:

> President of Ukraine Volodymyr Zelensky had a phone conversation with President of the United States Donald Trump. President of the United States congratulated Ukraine on successful holding free and

---

[61] Volker transcribed interview, *supra* note 60, at 102-03.

[62] *Impeachment Inquiry: Ambassador Kurt Volker and Timothy Morrison, supra* note 8.

[63] Sondland deposition, *supra* note 51, at 116.

[64] *Id.*

[65] Deposition of George Kent, in Wash., D.C., at 163 (Oct. 15, 2019) [hereinafter "Kent deposition"].

[66] *Id.* at 163-65

[67] Press Release, Office of the President of Ukraine, Volodymyr Zelenskyy had a phone conversation with President of the United States (July 25, 2019), *available at* https://www.president.gov.ua/en/news/volodimir-zelenskij-proviv-telefonnu-rozmovu-z-prezidentom-s-56617.

democratic parliamentary elections as well as Volodymyr Zelensky with victory the Servant of the People Party.

Donald Trump is convinced that the new Ukrainian government will be able to quickly improve image of Ukraine, complete investigation of corruption cases, which inhibited the interaction between Ukraine and the USA.

He also confirmed continued support of the sovereignty and territorial integrity of Ukraine by the United States and the readiness of the American side to fully contribute to the implementation of a Large-Scale Reform Program in our country.

Volodymyr Zelensky thanked Donald Trump for US leadership in preserving and strengthening the sanctions pressure on Russia.

The Presidents agreed to discuss practical issues of Ukrainian-American cooperation during the visit of Volodymyr Zelensky to the United States.[68]

The initial read-outs of the July 25 telephone conversation between President Trump and President Zelensky provide compelling evidence that the key message conveyed during the conversation was about fighting corruption in Ukraine—and not about digging up dirt on President Trump's political rival for the President's political benefit.

5. The National Security Council leadership did not see the call as illegal or improper.

The evidence shows that the NSC leadership did not see the telephone conversation between President Trump and President Zelensky as improper. Timothy Morrison, who served as the Deputy Assistant to the President for National Security, listened in on the conversation.[69] He testified that he was concerned information from the call could leak, but he was not concerned that anything discussed on the call was illegal or improper.[70]

LTG Keith Kellogg, Vice President Pence's National Security Advisor, also listened in on the July 25 telephone conversation.[71] LTG Kellogg stated that like Morrison: "I heard nothing wrong or improper on the call. I had and have no concerns."[72] LTG Kellogg's subordinate, Jennifer Williams, testified that although she found the call to be "unusual," she did not raise

---

[68] *Id.*

[69] Morrison deposition, *supra* note 12, at 15.

[70] *Id.* at 16, 60-61.

[71] The White House, Statement from Lieutenant General Keith Kellogg, National Security Advisor to Vice President Mike Pence (Nov. 19, 2019) [hereinafter "Statement from Lieutenant General Kellogg"].

[72] *Id.*

concerns to LTG Kellogg.[73] LTG Kellogg similarly noted that Williams never raised concerns to him.[74]

Morrison's subordinate, LTC Vindman, listened in on the conversation.[75] At the time of the call, LTC Vindman handled Ukraine policy for the NSC.[76] He testified that he was concerned by the conversation and raised his concerns to the NSC's Legal Advisor, John Eisenberg.[77] Eisenberg, according to LTC Vindman, did not share the concern.[78] LTC Vindman did not raise any concerns to Morrison, his immediate supervisor.[79] In his public testimony, Morrison explained that he had concerns with LTC Vindman's judgment and deviation from the chain of command.[80]

The evidence suggests that any wider concerns about the July 25 phone call originated from LTC Vindman. Williams testified that she discussed the call with no one outside the NSC.[81] LTC Vindman, on the other hand, testified that he discussed the phone call with two people outside of the NSC, Deputy Assistant Secretary Kent and an unidentified intelligence community employee.[82] Deputy Assistant Secretary Kent explained that LTC Vindman felt "uncomfortable" and would not share the majority of the substance of the conversation.[83] According to Kent's recollection, LTC Vindman did not mention that the conversation included any reference to Vice President Biden.[84]

6. The anonymous, secondhand whistleblower complaint misstated details about the July 25 call, which has falsely colored the call's public characterization.

The anonymous whistleblower did not listen in on the July 25 call between President Trump and President Zelensky. The whistleblower's subsequent complaint about the conversation, compiled with secondhand information, misstated key details about the conversation.

The whistleblower sensationally alleged that President Trump "sought to pressure the Ukrainian leader to take actions to help the President's 2020 reelection bid."[85] The call summary, however, contains no reference to 2020 or President Trump's reelection bid.[86]

---

[73] Deposition of Jennifer Williams, in Wash., D.C., at 129 (Nov. 7, 2019) [hereinafter "Williams deposition"]; *Impeachment Inquiry: LTC Alexander Vindman and Ms. Jennifer Williams, supra* note 6.
[74] Statement from Lieutenant General Kellogg, *supra* note 71.
[75] Vindman deposition, *supra* note 12, at 18.
[76] *Id.* at 16.
[77] *Id.* at 96.
[78] *Id.* at 97, 258.
[79] Morrison deposition, *supra* note 12, at 59.
[80] *Impeachment Inquiry: Ambassador Kurt Volker and Mr. Timothy Morrison, supra* note 8.
[81] *Impeachment Inquiry: LTC Alexander Vindman and Ms. Jennifer Williams, supra* note 6.
[82] *Id.*
[83] Kent deposition, *supra* note 65, at 163-64.
[84] *Id.* at 165-66.
[85] Letter to Richard Burr, Chairman, S. Sel. Comm. on Intelligence, & Adam Schiff, Chairman, H. Perm. Sel. Comm. on Intelligence 2 (Aug. 12, 2019) [hereinafter "Whistleblower letter"].
[86] *Memorandum of Telephone Conversation, supra* note 15.

The whistleblower alleged that President Trump "pressured" President Zelensky to "initiate or continue an investigation into the activities of former Vice President Joseph Biden and his son, Hunter Biden."[87] The call summary, however, shows that President Trump referenced the Bidens only in passing and that the presidents did not discuss the topic substantively.[88]

The whistleblower alleged that President Trump "pressured" President Zelensky to "locate and turn over servers used by the Democratic National Committee (DNC) and examined by the U.S. cyber security firm Crowdstrike."[89] The call summary, however, demonstrates that while President Trump mentioned Crowdstrike and "the server," President Trump never made any request that President Zelensky locate or turn over any material.[90]

The whistleblower alleged that President Trump "praised Ukraine's Prosecutor General, Mr. Yuriy Lutsenko, and suggested that Mr. Zelensky might want to keep him in his position."[91] The call summary is not clear about which prosecutor general President Trump is referring to— Ambassador Volker testified he believed President Trump was referring to Lutsenko's predecessor, Viktor Shokin[92]—and President Trump never specifically referenced Lutsenko.[93] President Trump also never suggested or intimated that President Zelensky should "keep [Lutsenko] in his position."[94]

The whistleblower also alleged that T. Ulrich Brechbuhl, Counselor to Secretary of State Mike Pompeo, listened in on the July 25 phone call.[95] Subsequent reporting, confirmed by a letter sent by Brechbuhl's attorney, indicated that Brechbuhl was not on the call.[96]

* * *

Setting aside the whistleblower's mischaracterization of President Trump's phone call with President Zelensky, the best available evidence shows no coercion, threats, or pressure for Ukraine to investigate the President's political rival for the President's political benefit. The call summary shows no *quid pro quo*, the initial read-outs relayed no substantive concerns, and both President Zelensky and President Trump have repeatedly said publicly there was no pressure. These facts refute the Democrats' allegations.

---

[87] Whistleblower letter, *supra* note 85, at 2.

[88] *Memorandum of Telephone Conversation*, *supra* note 15.

[89] Whistleblower letter, *supra* note 85, at 2.

[90] *Memorandum of Telephone Conversation*, *supra* note 15, at 3.

[91] Whistleblower letter, *supra* note 85, at 3.

[92] Volker transcribed interview, *supra* note 60, at 355.

[93] *Memorandum of Telephone Conversation*, *supra* note 15.

[94] *Id.*

[95] Whistleblower letter, *supra* note 85, at 3.

[96] Christina Ruffini (@EenaRuffini), Twitter (Sept. 26, 2019, 12:41 p.m.), https://twitter.com/EenaRuffini/status/1177307225024544768; Letter from Ronald Tenpas to Adam Schiff, Chairman, H. Perm. Sel. Comm. on Intelligence (Nov. 5, 2019).

B. The evidence does not establish that President Trump withheld a meeting with President Zelensky to pressure Ukraine to investigate the President's political rival for the purpose of benefiting him in the 2020 election.

Democrats allege that President Trump withheld a meeting with President Zelensky as a way of pressuring Ukraine to investigate President Trump's political rival.[97] Here, too, the evidence obtained during the impeachment inquiry does not support this allegation. President Trump and President Zelensky met *without* Ukraine ever investigating Vice Present Biden or his son, Hunter Biden.

The evidence strongly suggests, instead, that President Trump was reluctant to meet with President Zelensky for a different reason—Ukraine's long history of pervasive corruption and uncertainty about whether President Zelensky would break from this history and live up to his anti-corruption campaign platform. The Democrats' witnesses described how President Trump has a deep-seated and genuine skepticism of Ukraine due to its corruption and that the President's view was reasonable. Because of President Trump's skepticism and because President Zelensky was a first-time candidate with relatively untested views, Ukraine and U.S. officials sought to convince President Trump that President Zelensky was the "real deal" on reform. President Trump ultimately signed a letter to President Zelensky on May 29 inviting him to the White House.

Although there were several months between President Trump's invitation on May 29 and the bilateral meeting on September 25, the evidence does not show the delay was intentional or aimed at pressuring President Zelensky. The Democrats' witnesses described the difficulty in scheduling high-level meetings and how an anticipated presidential meeting in Poland in early September was cancelled due to Hurricane Dorian. Nonetheless, U.S. foreign policy officials believed that the Ukrainian government felt good about its relationship with the Trump Administration because of several high-level bilateral meetings held between May and September 2019, including President Zelensky's meeting with Vice President Pence on September 1. Ultimately, of course, President Trump and President Zelensky met during the U.N. General Assembly in New York on September 25, without Ukraine taking steps to investigate President Trump's political rival.

1. Ukraine has a long history of pervasive corruption.

Since it became an independent nation following the collapse of the Soviet Union, Ukraine has been plagued by systemic corruption. *The Guardian* has called Ukraine "the most corrupt nation in Europe"[98] and Ernst & Young cites Ukraine among the three most-corrupt nations of the world.[99]

---

[97] *See, e.g.*, Karoun Demirjian et al., *Officials' texts reveals belief that Trump wanted probes as condition of Ukraine meeting*, Wash. Post, Oct. 4, 2019.

[98] Oliver Bullough, *Welcome to Ukraine, the Most Corrupt Nation in Europe*, Guardian, (Feb. 6, 2015).

[99] *See, e.g.*, *14ᵗʰ Global Fraud Survey*, Ernst & Young, (2016), https://www.ey.com/Publication/vwLUAssets/EY-corporate-misconduct-individual-consequences/$FILE/EY-corporate-misconduct-individual-consequences.pdf (noting that 88% of Ukrainian's agree that "bribery/corrupt practices happen widely in business in [Ukraine]"). *See also* Viktor Tkachuk, *People First: The Latest in the Watch on Ukrainian Democracy*, Kyiv Post, (Sept. 11, 2012),

The United States Agency for International Development (USAID) explained Ukraine's history of corruption in a 2006 report:

> From the early 1990s, powerful officials in [the Ukrainian] government and politics acquired and privatized key economic resources of the state. As well, shadowy businesses, allegedly close to organized crime, became powerful economic forces in several regions of the country. Over the course of the past decade, these business groupings—or clans—as they became called, grew into major financial-industrial structures that used their very close links with and influence over government, political parties, the mass media and the state bureaucracy to enlarge and fortify their control over the economy and sources of wealth. They used ownership ties, special privileges, relations with government and direct influence over the courts and law enforcement and regulatory organizations to circumvent weaknesses in governmental institutions.[100]

Corruption is so pervasive in Ukraine that in 2011, 68.8% of Ukrainian citizens reported that they had bribed a public official within the preceding twelve months.[101] Bribery and facilitation payments[102] are common schemes by which Ukrainian officials demand payment in exchange for ensuring public services are delivered either on time or at all.[103] Corruption also presents an obstacle to private and public business in Ukraine.[104] In 2011, then-President Petro Poroshenko estimated that 15%, or $7.4 billion, of the state budget "ends up in the pockets of officials" through corrupt public procurement practices.[105]

Pervasive corruption in Ukraine has been one of the primary impediments to Ukraine joining the European Union.[106] Corruption-related concerns also figure prominently in the E.U.-Ukrainian Association Agreement, the document establishing a political and economic

---

https://www.kyivpost.com/article/opinion/op-ed/people-first-the-latest-in-the-watch-on-ukrainian-democracy-5-312797.html.

[100] U.S. Agency for International Development, Final Report, Corruption Assessment: Ukraine (2006), https://pdf.usaid.gov/pdf_docs/PNADK247.pdf.

[101] *Fighting Corruption in Ukraine: Ukrainian Style*, Gorshenin Inst., (Mar. 7, 2011), http://gpf-europe.com/upload/iblock/333/round_table_eng.pdf.

[102] *See* Facilitation Payments, *Corruption Dictionary*, Ganintegrity.com, (last visited Oct. 23, 2019), https://www.ganintegrity.com/portal/corruption-dictionary/. Facilitation payments, also known as "grease payments," are a form of bribery made with the purpose of expediting or securing the performance of a routine action to which the payer is legally entitled. *Id.*

[103] *People & Corruption: Citizens' Voices from Around the World*, Transparency Int'l, (2017), https://www.transparency.org/whatwedo/publication/people_and_corruption_citizens_voices_from_around_the_world.

[104] *Id.*

[105] Mark Rachkevych, *Under Yanukovych, Ukraine Slides Deeper in Ranks of Corrupt Nations*, Kyiv Post, (Dec. 1, 2011).

[106] *See, e.g.*, Vladimir Isachenkov, *Ukraine's integration into West dashed by war and corruption*, Assoc. Press, Mar. 26, 2019.

association between the E.U. and Ukraine.[107] The Agreement was entered into with the intent of Ukraine committing to gradually conform to E.U. technical and consumer standards.

State Department witnesses called by the Democrats during the impeachment inquiry confirmed Ukraine's reputation for corruption. Deputy Assistant Secretary of State George Kent described Ukraine's corruption problem as "serious" and said corruption has long been "part of the high-level dialogue" between the United States and Ukraine.[108] Ambassador Bill Taylor said corruption in Ukraine is a "big issue."[109] Ambassador Kurt Volker testified that "Ukraine has a long history of pervasive corruption throughout the economy[,] throughout the country, and it has been incredibly difficult for Ukraine as a country to deal with this, to investigate it, to prosecute it."[110] He later elaborated:

> Ukraine had for decades a reputation of being just a corrupt place. There are a handful of people who own a disproportionate amount of the economy. Oligarchs, they use corruption as kind of the coin of the realm to get what they want, including influencing the Parliament, the judiciary, the government, state-owned industries. And so businessmen generally don't want to invest in Ukraine, even to this day, because they just fear that it's a horrible environment to be working in, and they don't want to put – expose themselves to that risk. I would have to believe that President Trump would be aware of that general climate.[111]

2. President Trump has a deep-seated, genuine, and reasonable skepticism of Ukraine due to its history of pervasive corruption.

Multiple Democrat witnesses offered firsthand testimony of President Trump's skeptical view of Ukraine, as far back as September 2017. Ambassador Volker explained: "President Trump demonstrated that he had a very deeply rooted negative view of Ukraine based on past corruption. And that's a reasonable position. Most people who would know anything about Ukraine would think that."[112] He elaborated that the President's concern about Ukraine was genuine,[113] and that this concern contributed to a delay in the meeting with President Zelensky. He explained:

---

[107] E.U.-Ukraine Ass'n Agreement, art. 14, Mar. 21, 2014, 57 Off. J. of the E.U. L161/3 ("In their cooperation on justice, freedom and security, the Parties shall attach particular importance to the consolidation of the rule of law and the reinforcement of institutions at all levels in the areas of administration in general and law enforcement and the administration of justice in particular. Cooperation will, in particular, aim at strengthening the judiciary, improving its efficiency, safeguarding its independence and impartiality, and combating corruption. Respect for human rights and fundamental freedoms will guide all cooperation on justice, freedom and security.").

[108] Kent deposition, *supra* note 65 at 105, 151.

[109] Taylor deposition, *supra* note 47, at 86.

[110] Volker transcribed interview, *supra* note 60, at 76.

[111] *Id.* at 148-49.

[112] *Id.* at 30.

[113] *Id.* at 295.

So the issue as I understood it was this deep-rooted, skeptical view of Ukraine, a negative view of Ukraine, preexisting 2019, you know, going back. When I started this, I had one other meeting with President Trump and [then-Ukrainian] President Poroshenko. It was in September of 2017. And at that time he had a very skeptical view of Ukraine. So I know he had a very deep-rooted skeptical view. And my understanding at the time was that even though he agreed in the [May23] meeting that we had with him, say, okay, I'll invite him, he didn't really want to do it. And that's why the meeting kept being delayed and delayed. [114]

Other testimony confirms Ambassador Volker's statements. Former U.S. Ambassador to Ukraine Marie Yovanovitch confirmed the President's skepticism, saying that she observed it during President Trump's meeting with President Poroshenko in September 2017.[115] She testified:

> Q. Were you aware of the President's deep-rooted skepticism about Ukraine's business environment?
>
> A. Yes.
>
> Q. And what did you know about that?
>
> A. That he—I mean, he shared that concern directly with President Poroshenko in their first meeting in the Oval Office.[116]

Dr. Fiona Hill, NSC Senior Director for Europe, also testified that President Trump was "quite publicly" skeptical of Ukraine and that "everyone has expressed great concerns about corruption in Ukraine."[117] Catherine Croft, a former NSC director, similarly attested to President's Trump skepticism when she staffed President Trump for two Ukraine matters in 2017, explaining: "Throughout both, I heard, directly and indirectly, President Trump described Ukraine as a corrupt country."[118]

3. Senior Ukrainian government officials publicly attacked President Trump during the 2016 campaign.

President Trump's skepticism about Ukraine was compounded by statements made by senior Ukrainian government officials in 2016 that were critical of then-candidate Trump and supportive of his opponent, former Secretary of State Hillary Clinton. Although Democrats have attempted to discredit these assertions as "debunked," the statements by Ukrainian leaders speak

---

[114] *Id.* at 41.
[115] Deposition of Ambassador Marie Yovanovitch, in Wash., D.C., at 142 (Oct. 11, 2019).
[116] *Id.*
[117] Hill deposition, *supra* note 12, at 118.
[118] Croft deposition, *supra* note 60, at 14.

for themselves and shed light on President Trump's mindset when interacting with President Zelensky in 2019.

In August 2016, less than three months before the election, Valeriy Chaly, then-Ukrainian Ambassador to the United States, authored an op-ed in the Washington-based publication *The Hill* criticizing candidate Trump for comments he made about Russia's occupation of Crimea.[119] Ambassador Chaly wrote that candidate Trump's comments "have raised serious concerns in [Kyiv] and beyond Ukraine."[120] Although President Zelensky dismissed Ambassador Chaly on July 19, 2019,[121] the ambassador's op-ed remains on the website of the Ukrainian Embassy in the U.S. as of the date of this report.[122]

Later that month, the *Financial Times* published an article asserting that Trump's candidacy led "Kyiv's wider political leadership to do something they would never have attempted before: intervene, however indirectly, in a US election."[123] The article quoted Serhiy Leshchenko, a Ukrainian Member of Parliament, to detail how the Ukrainian government was supporting Secretary Clinton's candidacy.[124] The article explained:

> Though most Ukrainians are disillusioned with the country's current leadership for stalled reforms and lackluster anti-corruption efforts, Mr. Leshchenko said events of the past two years had locked Ukraine on to a pro-western course. ***The majority of Ukraine's politicians, he added, are "on Hillary Clinton's side."***[125]

The *Financial Times* reported that during the U.S. presidential campaign, former Ukrainian Prime Minister Arseniy Yatsenyuk had warned on Facebook that candidate Trump "challenged the very values of the free world."[126] On Twitter, Ukrainian Internal Affairs Minister Arsen Avakov called Trump a "clown" who is "an even bigger danger to the US than terrorism."[127] In a Facebook post, Avakov called Trump "dangerous for Ukraine and the US" and said that Trump's Crimea comments were the "diagnosis of a dangerous misfit."[128] Avakov continues to serve in President Zelensky's government.

Multiple Democrat witnesses testified that these Ukrainian actions during the 2016 election campaign likely also colored President Trump's views of President Zelensky. Ambassador Volker said:

---

[119] *See* Chaly, *supra* note 27.

[120] *Id.*

[121] *Zelensky dismisses Valeriy Chaly from post of Ukraine's envoy to US*, Kyiv Post (July 19, 2019).

[122] Embassy of Ukraine in the United States of America, *Op-ed by Ambassador of Ukraine to the USA Valeriy Chaly for the Hill: "Trump's comments send wrong message to world,"* https://usa.mfa.gov.ua/en/press-center/publications/4744-posol-ukrajini-vislovlyuvannya-trampa-nadsilajuty-nevirnij-signal-svitu.

[123] Roman Olearchyk, *Ukraine's leaders campaign against 'pro-Putin' Trump*, Financial Times, Aug. 28, 2016.

[124] *Id.*

[125] *Id.* (emphasis added).

[126] *Id.*

[127] Kenneth P. Vogel & David Stern, *Ukrainian efforts to sabotage Trump backfire*, Politico, Jan. 11, 2017.

[128] *Id.*

Q. And you mentioned that the President was skeptical, had a deep-rooted view of the Ukraine. Is that correct?

A. That is correct.

Q. And that, whether fair or unfair, he believed there were officials in Ukraine that were out to get him in the run-up to his election?

A. That is correct.

Q. So, to the extent there are allegations lodged, credible or uncredible, if the president was made aware of those allegations, whether it was via The Hill or, you know, via Mr. Giuliani or via cable news, if the President was made aware of these allegations, isn't it fair to say that he may, in fact, have believed they were credible?

A. Yes, I believe so.[129]

Ambassador Sondland similarly testified:

Q. Did [President Trump] mention anything about Ukraine's involvement in the 2016 election?

A. I think he said: They tried to take me down. He kept saying that over and over.

Q. In connection with the 2016 election?

A. Probably, yeah.

Q. That was what your understanding was?

A. That was my understanding, yeah.[130]

4. U.S. foreign policy officials were split on President Zelensky, a political novice with untested views on anti-corruption and a close relationship with a controversial oligarch.

Evidence obtained during the Democrats' impeachment inquiry shows that the U.S. foreign policy apparatus was divided on the question of whether President Trump should meet with President Zelensky. President Zelensky was a first-time candidate and a newcomer to the Ukrainian political scene. Although President Zelensky ran on an anti-corruption and reform platform, the Democrats' witnesses explained that the State Department was unsure how he

---

[129] Volker transcribed interview, *supra* note 60, at 70-71.
[130] Sondland deposition, *supra* note 51, at 75.

would govern as president. In addition, others in the U.S. government worried about President Zelensky's association with Ukrainian oligarch Igor Kolomoisky.

President Zelensky won a landslide victory on April 21, 2019, defeating incumbent President Petro Poroshenko by a 73-24 percent margin.[131] The win came as a surprise to many.[132] At the time of his election, Mr. Zelensky was a comedic television personality. Ambassador Volker testified that "Zelensky kind of came up out of nowhere. . . . When he arose kind of meteorically, as an outside figure and a popular candidate, I think it did take everybody by surprise."[133]

Ambassador Yovanovitch also testified that Zelensky's election came as a surprise. She explained:

> And I think that there was, you know, as is true, I think, probably in any country during Presidential elections, a lot of – a lot of concerns among people. This was I think a big surprise for the political elite of Ukraine, which is relatively small. And so, I don't think they saw it coming really until the very end. And, so, there was surprise and, you know, all the stages of grief, anger, disbelief, how is this happening?[134]

Ambassador Yovanovitch agreed that President Zelensky was an "untried" politician:

> Q. And how did you feel about [Zelensky winning the election]? What were your views of Zelensky? Did you think he was going to be a good advocate for the anticorruption initiatives, as he was campaigning on?
>
> A. We didn't know. I mean, he was an untried politician. Obviously, he has a background as a comedian, as an actor, as a businessperson, but we didn't know what he would be like as a President.[135]

Ambassador Sondland testified that there was a difference in opinion regarding whether to schedule a call between Presidents Trump and Zelensky. Ambassador Sondland recalled that he, Ambassador Volker, and Secretary Perry advocated for a call between the presidents, while NSC officials disagreed.[136]

Evidence suggests that U.S. officials had concerns about some people surrounding President Zelensky. Ambassador Volker testified that President Zelensky's chief of presidential administration, Andriy Bohdan, had earlier been an attorney for "a very famous oligarch in

[131] *Ukraine election: Comedian Zelensky wins presidency by landside*, BBC News (Apr. 22, 2019*)*.
[132] *Id.*
[133] Volker transcribed interview, *supra* note 60 at 152-53.
[134] Yovanovitch deposition, *supra* note 115, at 73-74.
[135] *Id.* at 74.
[136] Sondland note 51, at 27-28.

Ukraine."[137] Senator Ron Johnson, who attended President Zelensky's inauguration in May 2019, recalled "concern over rumors that [President] Zelensky was going to appoint Andriy Bohdan, the lawyer for oligarch Igor Kolomoisky, as his chief of staff. The delegation [to the inauguration] viewed Bohdan's rumored appointment to be contrary to the goal of fighting corruption and maintaining U.S. support."[138] President Zelensky appointed Bohdan to be head of presidential administration in May 2019.[139]

In addition, Dr. Hill explained that the NSC had a concern about President Zelensky's relationship with Kolomoisky, an oligarch who had owned the television station on which Zelensky's comedy show aired.[140] Under the Poroshenko regime, the Ukrainian government had accused Kolomoisky of embezzling from PrivatBank, which he co-owned, causing Kolomoisky to flee Ukraine.[141] According to Ambassador Volker, "the Ukrainian taxpayer officially is bailing out the bank for the money that Kolomoisky stole. Because the IMF provides budgetary support to Ukraine, we [the U.S. taxpayers] actually ended up bailing out this bank."[142]

Ambassador Taylor testified that he discussed these concerns about Kolomoisky directly with President Zelensky:

> [T]he influence of one particular oligarch over Mr. Zelensky is of particular concern, and that's this fellow Kolomoisky, so – and Kolomoisky has growing influence. And this is one of the concerns that I have expressed to President Zelensky and his team on several occasions very explicitly, saying that, you know, Mr. President, Kolomoisky was not elected. You were elected and he, Mr. Kolomoisky, is increasing his influence in your government, which could cause you to fail. So I've had that conversation with him a couple of times.[143]

Kolomoisky returned to Ukraine following President Zelensky's victory.[144]

5. President Trump extended an invitation to the White House to President Zelensky on three occasions without conditions.

The evidence demonstrates that President Trump had a deep skepticism of Ukraine based on its history of pervasive corruption. This inherent skepticism, coupled with certain Ukrainian government officials' criticism of candidate Trump during the 2016 campaign and President Zelensky's untested views, contributed to President Trump's reticence to meet with President

---

[137] Volker transcribed interview, *supra* note 60, at 137.

[138] Letter from Sen. Ron Johnson to Jim Jordan, Ranking Member, H. Comm. on Oversight & Reform, & Devin Nunes, Ranking Member, H. Perm. Sel. Comm. on Intelligence 3 (Nov. 18, 2019).

[139] Roman Olearchyk, *Volodymyr Zelensky hires oligarch's lawyer as chief of staff*, Financial Times, May 22, 2019.

[140] Hill deposition, *supra* note 12, at 76-77.

[141] Andrew E. Kramer, *Oligarch's return raises alarm in Ukraine*, N.Y. Times, May 16, 2019.

[142] Volker transcribed interview, *supra* note 60, at 246.

[143] Taylor deposition, *supra* note 47, at 86.

[144] Kramer, *supra* note 141.

Zelensky. In spring and summer 2019, however, the President extended an invitation to the White House to President Zelensky on three occasions—without any conditions.

On April 21, 2019, President Trump placed a brief congratulatory call to President-elect Zelensky.[145] President Trump said: "When you're settled in and ready, I'd like to invite you to the White House."[146] The presidents did not discuss any investigations, and President Trump placed no conditions on his invitation.

On May 23, President Trump met with Ambassador Volker, Ambassador Sondland, Secretary Perry, and Senator Johnson—the senior U.S. officials who had comprised the official U.S. delegation to President Zelensky's inauguration days before. The delegation sought to convey to President Trump a positive impression of President Zelensky.[147] According to Ambassador Volker:

> President Trump demonstrated that he had a very deeply rooted negative view of Ukraine based on past corruption. And that's a reasonable position. Most people who would know anything about Ukraine would think that. That's why it was important that we wanted to brief him, because we were saying, it's different, this guy is different. But the President had a very deeply rooted negative view. We urged that he invite President Zelensky to meet with him at the White House. He was skeptical of that. We persisted. And he finally agreed, okay, I'll do it.[148]

Later in his transcribed interview, Ambassador Volker provided more context for the May 23 discussion:

> What I heard from President Trump in the meeting in the oval office was blanket, like, "this—these are terrible people, this is a corrupt country," you know, "I don't believe it." I made the argument that President Zelensky is the real deal, he is going to try to fix things, and, you know, he just did not believe it. He waved it off. So there's a general issue there.
>
> He did not mention investigations to me in that meeting, or call for investigations. I was not aware that he did so in the July 25th call later. His attitude towards Ukraine was just general and negative.[149]

Ambassador Sondland similarly testified that President Trump expressed negative views about Ukraine in this meeting and mentioned how "they tried to take me down" in 2016.[150]

---

[145] *Memorandum of Telephone Conversation, supra* note 10.
[146] *Id.*
[147] Hill deposition, *supra* note 12, at 320.
[148] Volker transcribed interview, *supra* note 60, at 30-31.
[149] *Id.* at 280.
[150] Sondland deposition, *supra* note 51, at 74-75.

Although Ambassador Sondland said he was discouraged by the President's viewpoint, he was pleased and surprised that the President later agreed to invite President Zelensky to the White House.[151]

Senator Johnson recalled that in this meeting, President Trump "expressed strong reservations about support for Ukraine. He made it crystal clear that he viewed Ukraine as a thoroughly corrupt country both generally and, specifically, regarding rumored meddling in the 2016 election."[152] Senator Johnson further explained:

> It was obvious that [the President's] viewpoint and reservations were strongly held, and that we would have a significant sales job ahead of us in getting him to change his mind. I specifically asked him to keep his viewpoint and reservations private and not to express them publicly until he had a chance to meet [President] Zelensky. He agreed to do so, but he added that he wanted [President] Zelensky to know exactly how he felt about the corruption in Ukraine prior to any future meeting.[153]

Senator Johnson recounted that he did not recall President Trump mentioning Burisma or the Bidens, but it was "obvious" that President Trump was aware of "rumors that corrupt actors in Ukraine might have played a part in helping create the false Russia collusion narrative."[154]

On May 29, President Trump wrote to President Zelensky to invite him to Washington, D.C. "as soon as we can find a mutually convenient time."[155] President Trump's letter did not mention any investigations and placed no conditions on President Zelensky's invitation to the White House. On July 25, during their phone conversation, President Trump reiterated his invitation to President Zelensky, again without conditions.[156]

6. **Despite difficulty scheduling a face-to-face presidential meeting, senior Ukrainian officials interacted often with senior American officials between May and September 2019.**

By late May 2019, President Trump had formally extended an invitation for President Zelensky to visit the White House. Although the two presidents did not meet face-to-face until September 25, the Democrats' witnesses testified that presidential meetings can often take time to schedule and that senior Ukrainian officials met frequently with American counterparts in the

---

[151] *Id.* at 74, 81, 85-87.

[152] Letter from Sen. Ron Johnson, *supra* note 138, at 4.

[153] *Id.*

[154] *Id.*

[155] Letter from President Donald J. Trump to His Excellency Volodymyr Zelenskyy, President of Ukraine (May 29, 2019). Dr. Hill testified that Ambassador Sondland claimed he had dictated the paragraph inviting President Zelensky to the White House, *see* Hill deposition, *supra* note 12, at 74; however, Ambassador Sondland testified that he had no role in drafting the letter. Sondland deposition, *supra* note 51, at 81.

[156] *Memorandum of Telephone Conversation, supra* note 15.

interim.[157] Ambassador Volker explained that the new Zelensky regime was "actually feeling pretty good by then" about its relationship with the Trump Administration.[158]

On June 4, President Zelensky attended an Independence Day dinner at the U.S. mission to the E.U. hosted by Ambassador Sondland and also attended by White House Senior Advisor Jared Kushner.[159]

On July 3, while in Toronto, Canada, for the Ukraine Reform Conference, President Zelensky met with Ambassador Volker and Deputy Assistant Secretary of State George Kent.[160]

On July 9, Oleksandr Danylyuk, then-Secretary of the National Security and Defense Council of Ukraine, and Andrey Yermak, a senior adviser to President Zelensky, met with LTG Keith Kellogg, Vice President Pence's National Security Advisor; Jennifer Williams, a special advisor covering European issues for Vice President Pence; and NSC staff member LTC Alexander Vindman.[161]

On July 10, Danylyuk and Yermak met at the White House with National Security Advisor John Bolton, Secretary Perry, Ambassador Volker, Ambassador Sondland, Dr. Hill, and LTC Vindman.[162]

On July 25, President Trump and President Zelensky spoke by telephone.[163]

On July 26, President Zelensky met with Ambassador Volker, Ambassador Sondland, and Ambassador Taylor in Kyiv.[164] Ambassador Volker testified that the meeting was scheduled before the presidents' phone call.[165] He said President Zelensky was "pleased that the call had taken place . . . . They thought it went well. And they were encouraged again because the President had asked them to pick dates for coming to the White House."[166]

On August 27, President Zelensky met with National Security Advisor Bolton in Kyiv.[167]

On September 1, President Zelensky met with Vice President Pence in Warsaw, Poland, after an event commemorating the 80th anniversary of the beginning of World War II.[168] President Trump had been scheduled to attend but was forced to cancel due to Hurricane

---

[157] Kent deposition, *supra* note 65, at 231; Volker transcribed interview, *supra* note 60, at 127.

[158] Volker transcribed interview, *supra* note 60, at 127.

[159] Sondland deposition, *supra* note 51, at 26-27, 148-49.

[160] Kent deposition, *supra* note 65, at 241; Volker transcribed interview, *supra* note 60, at 137.

[161] Williams deposition, *supra* note 73, at 51-53.

[162] Volker transcribed interview, *supra* note 60, at 66-67; Hill deposition, *supra* note 12, at 62-63.

[163] *Memorandum of Telephone Conversation, supra* note 15.

[164] Volker transcribed interview, *supra* note 60, at 312-33; Sondland deposition, *supra* note 51, at 29.

[165] Volker transcribed interview, *supra* note 60, at 102.

[166] *Id.* at 313.

[167] Taylor deposition, *supra* note 47, at 229-30.

[168] The White House, Readout of Vice President Mike Pence's Meeting with Ukrainian President Volodymyr Zelenskyy (Sept. 1, 2019); Taylor deposition, *supra* note 47, at 34-35.

Dorian.[169] According to Ambassador Taylor's testimony, Vice President Pence reiterated President Trump's views for "Europeans to do more to support Ukraine and that he wanted the Ukrainians to do more to fight corruption."[170]

On September 17, Secretary of State Pompeo had a telephone conversation with Ukrainian Foreign Minister Vadym Prystaiko.[171] According to a readout from the U.S. Embassy in Kyiv, Secretary Pompeo "affirmed U.S. support for Ukraine as it advances critical reforms to tackle corruption, strengthen the rule of law, and foster an economic environment that promotes competition and investment. The Secretary expressed unwavering U.S. support for Ukraine's sovereignty and territorial integrity."[172]

On September 18, President Zelensky and Vice President Pence spoke by telephone.[173] The two discussed President Zelensky's upcoming meeting with President Trump on the margins of the U.N. General Assembly and Ukraine's effort to address its corruption challenges.[174]

7. The evidence does not establish a linkage between a White House meeting and Ukrainian investigations into President Trump's political rival.

The evidence in the Democrats' impeachment inquiry does not show that a White House meeting was conditioned on Ukraine's willingness to investigate President Trump's political rival. Although the anonymous whistleblower, citing "multiple" secondhand sources, alleged that President Trump sought to withhold a meeting to pressure President Zelensky to "play ball,"[175] publicly available information contradicts the whistleblower's claim. For example, Andrey Yermak, a senior adviser to President Zelensky, admitted in an August 2019 *New York Times* article that he discussed with Mayor Giuliani both meeting between President Trump and President Zelensky and investigations.[176] The *Times* reported, however, that Yermak and Mayor Giuliani "did not discuss a link between the two."[177]

Other firsthand testimony obtained during the impeachment inquiry supports this finding. For example, Ambassador Volker, the key interlocutor with the Ukrainian government, clearly testified that there was no "linkage" between a White House meeting and Ukrainian actions to investigate President Trump's political rival. He explained:

> Q. Did the President ever withhold a meeting with President Zelensky until the Ukrainians committed to investigating those allegations?

---

[169] Volker transcribed interview, *supra* note 60, at 130; Taylor deposition, *supra* note 47, at 35.

[170] Taylor deposition, *supra* note 47, at 35.

[171] U.S. Embassy in Ukraine, Secretary Michael R. Pompeo's Call with Ukrainian Foreign Minister Vadym Prystayko (Sept. 17, 2019), https://ua.usembassy.gov/secretary-michael-r-pompeos-call-with-ukrainian-foreign-minister-vadym-prystayko/.

[172] *Id.*

[173] The White House, Readout of Vice President Mike Pence's Phone Call with President of Ukraine (Sept. 18, 2019).

[174] *Id.*; *see also* Volker transcribed interview, *supra* note 60, at 317-18.

[175] Whistleblower letter, *supra* note 85, at 7.

[176] Kenneth P. Vogel & Andrew E. Kramer, *Giuliani renews push for Ukraine to investigate Trump's political opponents*, N.Y. Times, Aug. 21, 2019.

[177] *Id.*

A. We had a difficult time scheduling a bilateral meeting between President Zelensky and President Trump.

Q. Ambassador Volker, that was a yes-or-no question.

A. Well, if I – can you repeat the question then?

Q. Sure. Did President Trump ever withhold a meeting with President Zelensky or delay a meeting with President Zelensky until the Ukrainians committed to investigate the allegations that you just described concerning the 2016 Presidential election?

A. The answer to the question is no, if you want a yes-or-no answer. But the reason the answer is no is we did have difficulty scheduling a meeting, but there was no linkage like that.[178]

***

Q. So before we move to the text messages, I want to ask you a clarifying question. You said that you were not aware of any linkage between the delay in the Oval Office meeting between President Trump and President Zelensky and the Ukrainian commitment to investigate the two allegations as you described them, correct?

A. Correct.[179]

Ambassador Sondland was the only witness to allege a *quid pro quo* with respect to a White House meeting. However, to the extent that Ambassador Sondland testified that he believed a White House meeting was conditioned on Ukrainian actions, his belief was that a meeting was conditioned on a public statement about anti-corruption—not on investigations into President Trump's political rival.[180] Ambassador Sondland testified in his closed-door deposition that "nothing about the request raised any red flags for me, Ambassador Volker, or Ambassador Taylor."[181] In his public testimony, Ambassador Sondland clarified that he *believed* there was linkage, but that President Trump had never discussed with him any preconditions for a White House visit by President Zelensky.[182]

In addition, there is conflicting testimony about what occurred during a July 10 meeting between two senior Ukrainian officials and senior U.S. officials in National Security Advisor John Bolton's office. Ambassador Volker, Ambassador Sondland, Secretary Perry joined

---

[178] Volker transcribed interview, *supra* note 60, at 35-36.
[179] *Id.* at 40.
[180] Sondland deposition, *supra* note 51, at 30, 331.
[181] *Id.* at 30.
[182] *Impeachment Inquiry: Ambassador Gordon Sondland, supra* note 56.

Ambassador Bolton to meet with Oleksandr Danylyuk, then-Secretary of Ukraine's National Security and Defense Council, and Andrey Yermak, an adviser to President Zelensky.[183] Dr. Hill and LTC Vindman from the NSC staff attended as well.[184]

Dr. Hill and LTC Vindman alleged that during the meeting, Ambassador Sondland raised potential Ukrainian actions on investigations, leading Ambassador Bolton to abruptly end the meeting.[185] Dr. Hill recounted that Ambassador Bolton told her to brief the NSC Legal Advisor, John Eisenberg, and said he would not be a part of what he termed a "drug deal."[186]

Although Dr. Hill testified that she confronted Ambassador Sondland over his discussion of investigations,[187] Ambassador Sondland testified in his closed-door deposition that "neither Ambassador Bolton, Dr. Hill, or anyone else on the NSC staff ever expressed any concerns to me about our efforts . . . or, most importantly, any concerns that we were acting improperly."[188] Ambassador Sondland testified in his deposition that he recalled no "unpleasant conversation" with Dr. Hill.[189] Likewise, although Ambassador Volker assessed that the meeting was "not good," he said it was because Danylyuk poorly conveyed the appropriate top-level message to Ambassador Bolton during the meeting.[190]

In his public testimony, Ambassador Volker acknowledged that Ambassador Sondland made a "general comment about investigations," but he disputed that the July 10 meeting ended abruptly.[191] He also testified that preconditions were not discussed during the meeting.[192] Although Ambassador Sondland denied in his closed-door depositions that he raised investigations during July 10 meeting,[193] he acknowledged that he did in his public testimony.[194] Even still, Ambassador Sondland denied that the July 10 meeting ended abruptly: "I don't recall any abrupt ending of the meeting or people storming out or anything like that. That would have been very memorable if someone had stormed out of a meeting, based on something I said."[195] He explained that Dr. Hill never raised concerns to him, and that any discussion of investigations did not mention specific investigations.[196] He testified:

> Q. And, in fact, after the meeting, you went out and you took a picture, right?

---

[183] Sondland deposition, *supra* note 51, at 27; Volker transcribed interview, *supra* note 60, at 50-51.

[184] Hill deposition, *supra* note 12, at 63; Vindman deposition, *supra* note 12, at 17-18.

[185] Hill deposition, *supra* note 12, at 67; Vindman deposition, *supra* note 12, at 17.

[186] Hill deposition, *supra* note 12, at 70-71.

[187] *Id.* at 68-71. Dr. Hill testified that she also had a "blow up" with Ambassador Sondland in June about Ukraine, saying that Ambassador Sondland got "testy." *Id.* at 113.

[188] Sondland deposition, *supra* note 51, at 28.

[189] *Id.* at 114.

[190] Volker transcribed interview, *supra* note 60, at 66.

[191] *Impeachment Inquiry: Ambassador Kurt Volker and Mr. Timothy Morrison, supra* note 8.

[192] *Id.*

[193] *Id.* at 109-10.

[194] *Impeachment Inquiry: Ambassador Gordon Sondland, supra* note 56.

[195] *Id.*

[196] *Id.*

A. Yeah. We – Ambassador Bolton – or his assistant indicated that he was out of time, that he needed – he had another meeting to attend. And we all walked out of the White House. Everyone was smiling, everyone was happy, and we took a picture on the lawn on a nice sunny day.

Q. Okay. Then did you retire to the Ward Room?

A. I think Secretary Perry asked to use the Ward Room to continue the conversation. And the real subject that was under debate – and it wasn't an angry debate, it was a debate – should the call from President Trump to President Zelensky be made prior to the parliamentary elections in Ukraine or after the parliamentary elections? And there was good reason for both. We felt – Ambassador Perry, Ambassador Volker, and I thought it would help President Zelensky to have President Trump speak to him prior to the parliamentary elections, because it would give President Zelensky more credibility, and ultimately he would do better with his people in the parliamentary elections. Others, I believe, pushed back and said, no, it's not appropriate to do it before. It should be done after. And ultimately, it was done after.

Q. Okay. There was no mention of Vice President Biden in the Ward Room?

A. Not that I remember, no.

Q. Or any specific investigation?

A. Just the generic investigations.[197]

Contemporaneous evidence contradicts the idea that there was serious discord during the meeting. Following the meeting, Ambassador Bolton retweeted a statement from Secretary Perry about the July 10 meeting, writing it was a "great discussion . . . on U.S. support for Ukrainian reforms and the peaceful restoration of Ukrainian territory."[198] The picture in the tweet of the U.S. and Ukrainian officials—taken immediately after the meeting in Ambassador Bolton's office[199]—shows smiling faces and no indication of hostility or discord between Ambassador Bolton and Ambassador Sondland.

---

[197] *Id.*
[198] John Bolton (@AmbJohnBolton), Twitter (July 10, 2019, 4:39 p.m.), https://twitter.com/AmbJohnBolton/status/1149100798632026112.
[199] Sondland deposition, *supra* note 51, at 110.

Figure 1: Ambassador Bolton tweet following July 10 meeting

Figure 2: Picture of smiling U.S. and Ukrainian officials following July 10 meeting

8. The evidence does not establish that President Trump directed Vice President Pence not to attend President Zelensky's inauguration to pressure Ukraine to investigate the President's political rival.

The evidence also does not establish that President Trump directed Vice President Pence not to attend President Zelensky's inauguration as a means of pressuring Ukraine to investigate the President's political rival. During their initial April 21 phone call, President Trump told President Zelensky that a "great" representative of the U.S. would attend the Zelensky inauguration.[200] The anonymous whistleblower alleged that President Trump later "instructed Vice President Pence to cancel his planned travel to Ukraine to attend President Zelensky's

---

[200] Memorandum of Telephone Conversation, *supra* note 10.

inauguration . . . . [I]t was also 'made clear' to them that the President did not want to meet with Mr. Zelensky until he saw how Zelensky 'chose to act' in office."[201] The evidence in the Democrats' impeachment inquiry does not support this assertion.

Although Jennifer Williams, a special adviser in the Office of the Vice President, testified in her closed-door deposition that a colleague told her that President Trump directed Vice President Pence not to attend the inauguration,[202] she had no firsthand knowledge of any such direction or the reasons given for any such direction.[203] Williams explained that the Office of the Vice President provided three dates—May 30, May 31 and June 1—during which Vice President Pence would be available to attend the inauguration.[204] Williams explained that "if it wasn't one of those dates it would be very difficult or impossible" for Vice President Pence to attend.[205] Neither the Secret Service nor advance teams deployed to Ukraine to prepare for Vice President Pence's travel.[206]

During this same period, Vice Present Pence was planning travel to Ottawa, Canada, on May 30 to promote the U.S.-Mexico-Canada Agreement (USMCA).[207] Williams acknowledged in her public testimony that the Office of the Vice President had "competing trips . . . for the same window."[208] Williams elaborated that due to international travel by President Trump and Vice President Pence, there was a "narrow window" within which Vice President Pence was able to attend President Zelensky's inauguration.[209] Dr. Hill explained that the President and Vice President cannot travel internationally at the same time, testifying that Vice President Pence's attendance at President Zelensky's inauguration was just dependent on scheduling and she had no knowledge that the Vice President was directed not to attend the inauguration.[210]

Ultimately, on May 16, the Ukrainian Parliament scheduled President Zelensky's inauguration for only four days later, May 20, which was a date not offered by the Vice President's Office.[211] Williams testified that this scheduling posed a problem: "To be honest, we hadn't looked that closely at the Vice President's schedule before the President's trip [to Japan]

---

[201] Whistleblower letter, *supra* note 85, at app. 1-2.

[202] Williams deposition, *supra* note 73, at 37.

[203] *Impeachment Inquiry: LTC Alexander Vindman and Ms. Jennifer Williams, supra* note 6.

[204] Williams deposition, *supra* note 73, at 58; *Impeachment Inquiry: LTC Alexander Vindman and Ms. Jennifer Williams, supra* note 6.

[205] Williams deposition, *supra* note 73, at 58.

[206] *Id.* at 59.

[207] *See* The White House, Joint Statement by Vice President Mike Pence and Canadian Prime Minister Justin Trudeau (May 30, 2019).

[208] *Impeachment Inquiry: LTC Alexander Vindman and Ms. Jennifer Williams, supra* note 6.

[209] *Id.*

[210] *"Impeachment Inquiry: Dr. Fiona Hill and Mr. David Holmes": Hearing before the H. Perm. Sel. Comm. on Intelligence,* 116th Cong. (2019); Hill deposition, *supra* note 12, at 185 ("It depended on the date. I mean, we were hoping, you know, if others couldn't attend that [Vice President Pence] could. I mean, I myself couldn't attend because of the date, that the way that it – again, there were several different dates, and then the date that was announced in May was very quickly announced."); *id.* at 316 ("And it was going to be very tight for the Vice President to make it for the inauguration. So, I, you know, have no knowledge that he was actually ordered not to go, but it was going to be very difficult for him to go.").

[211] Kent deposition, *supra* note 65, at 189.

at the end of May just because we weren't expecting the Ukrainians to look at that timeframe."[212] Kent explained that this short notice sent the State Department "scrambl[ing]" to find a U.S. official to lead the delegation.[213] Secretary Pompeo was traveling, so the decision was made to ask Secretary Perry to lead the delegation.[214] On May 20, the day of President Zelensky's inauguration, Vice President Pence attended an event in Jacksonville, Florida, to promote the USMCA.[215]

9. **President Trump and President Zelensky met during the United Nations General Assembly in September 2019 without any Ukrainian action to investigate President Trump's political rival.**

On September 25, President Trump and President Zelensky met during the U.N. General Assembly in New York.[216] Ambassador Volker said that President Trump and President Zelensky had a "positive" meeting. He testified:

> Q. Turning back to President Trump's skepticism of Ukraine and the corruption there, do you think you made any inroads in convincing him that Zelensky was a good partner?
>
> A. I do. I do. I attended the President's meeting with President Zelensky in New York on, I guess it was the 25th of September. And I could see the body language and the chemistry between them was positive, and I felt that this is what we needed all along.[217]

Ambassador Taylor testified that the meeting was "good" and President Trump "left pleased that they had finally met face to face."[218] Ambassador Taylor said there was no discussion about investigations during the September 25 meeting.[219]

Notably, President Trump and President Zelensky met in New York without Ukraine ever investigating President Trump's political rival.

* * *

The evidence presented in the impeachment inquiry does not support the Democrats' assertion that President Trump sought to withhold a White House meeting to pressure the Ukrainian government to investigate the President's political rival. President Trump and President Zelensky met in September 2019 *without* Ukraine ever investigating Vice President Biden or Hunter Biden.

---

[212] Williams deposition, *supra* note 73, at 60.
[213] Kent deposition, *supra* note 65, at 190.
[214] *Id.* at 190-91.
[215] The White House, Remarks by Vice President Pence at America First Policies Event USMCA: A Better Deal for American Worker (May 20, 2019).
[216] Remarks by President Trump and President Zelensky of Ukraine Before Bilateral Meeting, *supra* note 40.
[217] Volker transcribed interview, *supra* note 60, at 87-88.
[218] Taylor deposition, *supra* note 47, at 288.
[219] *Id.*

Contrary to the assertions in the anonymous whistleblower complaint, the evidence shows that President Trump has a genuine, deep-seated, and reasonable skepticism of Ukraine given its history of pervasive corruption. In addition, U.S. foreign policy officials were divided on whether President Trump should meet with President Zelensky, in part due to President Zelensky's close association with an oligarch accused of embezzlement. In May 2019, President Trump formally invited President Zelensky to the White House. For several months, there were attempts to arrange a meeting between President Trump and President Zelensky. Although President Trump indicated during their July 25 call that they may meet in Warsaw in September, Hurricane Dorian forced President Trump to cancel. Vice President Pence met with President Zelensky instead. President Trump and President Zelensky ultimately met without Ukraine ever investigating any of President Trump's political rival.

C. The evidence does not establish that President Trump withheld U.S. security assistance to Ukraine to pressure Ukraine to investigate the President's political rival for the purpose of benefiting him in the 2020 election.

Democrats allege that President Trump conspired to withhold U.S. security assistance to Ukraine as a way of pressuring Ukraine to investigate President Trump's political rival.[220] Here, too, the evidence obtained during the impeachment inquiry does not support this allegation.

The evidence suggests a far less nefarious reality. Just as President Trump holds a deep-seated skepticism about Ukraine, the President is highly skeptical of foreign assistance. Any examination of the President's actions must consider this factor. President Trump has been vocal about his view that U.S. allies in Europe should contribute a fair share for regional security. As Ukrainian government officials worked with U.S. officials to convince President Trump that President Zelensky was serious about reform and worthy of U.S. assistance, they discussed a public statement conveying that commitment. Although the security assistance was paused in July, it is not unusual for U.S. foreign assistance to become delayed. Assistance to Ukraine has been delayed before. Most telling, the Trump Administration has been stronger than the Obama Administration in providing Ukraine with lethal defensive arms to deter Russian aggression.

The Democrats' witnesses testified that U.S. security assistance to Ukraine was not conditioned on Ukrainian action on investigations. U.S. officials did not raise the issue of the delay in security assistance with Ukrainian officials because they viewed it as a bureaucratic issue that would be resolved. The Ukrainian government in Kyiv was not even aware that the aid was paused until it was reported publicly, only two weeks before the aid was released, as senior U.S. officials confidently predicted it would be. Ultimately, the U.S. disbursed security assistance to Ukraine *without* Ukraine ever investigating Vice Present Biden or his son, Hunter Biden.

---

[220] *See, e.g.*, Rishika Dugyala, *Democratic Senator: 'No doubt' Ukraine 'felt pressure'*, Politico (Oct. 27, 2019).

1. President Trump has been skeptical about U.S. taxpayer-funded foreign assistance.

Evidence suggests that President Trump is generally skeptical of U.S. taxpayer-funded foreign assistance. President Trump's skepticism of U.S. taxpayer-funded foreign assistance is long-standing. On June 16, 2015, when President Trump announced his candidacy for president, he said:

> It is time to stop sending jobs overseas through bad foreign trade deals. We will renegotiate our trade deals with the toughest negotiators our country has… the ones who have actually read "The Art of the Deal" and know how to make great deals for our country.
>
> It is time to close loopholes for Wall Street and create far more opportunities for small businesses.
>
> It is necessary that we invest in our infrastructure, *stop sending foreign aid to countries that hate us and use that money to rebuild our tunnels, roads, bridges and schools—and nobody can do that better than me.*[221]

During the 2016 presidential campaign, then-candidate Trump continued to express his skepticism of U.S. taxpayer-funded foreign aid. In March 2016, he told the *Washington Post*, "I do think it's a different world today and I don't think we should be nation building anymore. I think it's proven not to work. And we have a different country than we did then. You know we have 19 trillion dollars in debt. . . . And I just think we have to rebuild our country."[222] That same month, then-candidate Trump told the *New York Times*, "We're going to be friendly with everybody, but we're not going to be taken advantage of by anybody. . . . I think we'll be very worldview [*sic*], but we're not going to be ripped off anymore by all of these countries."[223]

As president, President Trump has sought to reduce U.S. taxpayer-funded foreign assistance. In his fiscal year 2018 budget proposal, the President proposed "to reduce or end direct funding for international programs and organizations whose missions do not substantially advance U.S. foreign policy interests. The Budget also renews attention on the appropriate U.S. share of international spending . . . for many other global issues where the United States currently pays more than its fair share."[224] The President's 2020 budget proposal—submitted in March 2019—likewise "supports America's reliable allies, but reflects a new approach toward countries that have taken unfair advantage of the United States' generosity."[225] The President's

---

[221] Donald Trump, Announcement of Candidacy for President of the United States, in New York, N.Y. (June 16, 2015) (emphasis added).

[222] *A transcript of Donald Trump's meeting with the Washington Post editorial board*, Wash. Post, Mar. 21, 2016.

[223] Maggie Haberman & David Sanger, *Transcript: Donald Trump Expounds on His Foreign Policy Views*, N.Y. Times, Mar. 26, 2016.

[224] Budget of the U.S. Government Fiscal Year 2018 at 13 (May 23, 2017).

[225] Budget of the U.S. Government Fiscal Year 2020 at 71 (Mar. 11, 2019).

Budget specifically sought "greater accountability by international partners along with donor burden sharing that is more balanced."[226]

Testimony from the Democrats' witnesses reinforces the President's skepticism of foreign assistance. Ambassador Taylor, U.S. chargé *a.i.* in Kyiv, testified that on August 22, 2019, he had a phone conversation with NSC Senior Director for Europe Tim Morrison in which Morrison said that the "President doesn't want to provide any assistance at all."[227] Morrison testified that President Trump generally does not like giving foreign aid to other countries and believes U.S. "ought not" to be the only country providing security assistance.[228] LTC Vindman, the NSC director handling Ukraine policy, similarly testified that President Trump is skeptical of foreign aid.[229]

In fact, evidence suggests that President Trump sought to review U.S. taxpayer-funded foreign assistance across the board. Ambassador David Hale, the Under Secretary of State for Political Affairs, testified that the Trump Administration was undertaking a "review" of foreign assistance globally.[230] He testified:

> Q. You mentioned that there was a foreign assistance review undergoing –
>
> A. Yes.
>
> Q. – at that time. What can you tell us about that?
>
> A. Well, it had been going on for quite a while, and the concept, you know, the administration did not want to take a, sort of, business-as-usual approach to foreign assistance, a feeling that once a country has received a certain assistance package, it's a – it's something that continues forever. It's very difficult to end those programs and to make sure that we have a very rigorous measure of why we are providing the assistance.
>
> We didn't go to zero base, but almost a zero-based concept that each assistance program and each country that receives the program had to be evaluated that they were actually worthy beneficiaries of our assistance; that the program made sense; that we have embarked on, you know, calling everything that we do around the world countering violent extremism, but, rather, that's actually focused on tangible and proven means to deal with extremist problems; that we avoid nation-building strategies; and that we not provide assistance to countries that are lost to us in terms of policy, to our adversaries.

---

[226] *Id.* at 73.

[227] Taylor deposition, *supra* note 47, at 33.

[228] Morrison deposition, *supra* note 12, at 78-79, 132.

[229] *Impeachment Inquiry: LTC Alexander Vindman and Ms. Jennifer Williams, supra* note 6.

[230] Deposition of Ambassador David Hale, in Wash., D.C., at 80 (Nov. 6, 2019) [hereinafter "Hale deposition"].

Q. And do you know if the President also had concerns about whether the allies of Ukraine, in this example, were contributing their fair share?

A. That's another factor in the foreign affairs review is appropriate burden sharing. But it was not, in the deputies committee meeting, OMB [the U.S. Office of Management and Budget] did not really explain why they were taking the position other than they had been directed to do so.

Q. Okay. You are aware of the President's skeptical views on foreign assistance? Right?

A. Absolutely.

Q. And that's a genuinely held belief, correct?

A. It is what guided the foreign affairs review.

Q. Okay. It's not just related to Ukraine?

A. Absolutely not. It's global in nature.[231]

2. President Trump has been clear and consistent in his view that Europe should pay its fair share for regional defense.

Since his 2016 presidential campaign, President Trump has emphasized his view that U.S. foreign assistance should be spent wisely and cautiously. As President, he has continued to be critical of sending U.S. taxpayer dollars to foreign countries and asked our allies to share the financial burden for international stewardship.

In a March 2016 interview with the *New York Times*, then-candidate Trump said: "Now, I'm a person that—you notice I talk about economics quite a bit [in foreign policy] because it is about economics, because we don't have money anymore because we've been taking care of so many people in so many different forms that we don't have money."[232] Then-candidate Trump elaborated about the North Atlantic Treaty Organization (NATO), a collective defense alliance between the U.S., Canada, and European countries:

> I mean, we defend everybody. (Laughs.) We defend everybody. No matter who it is, we defend everybody. We're defending the world. But we owe, soon, it's soon to be $21 trillion. You know, it's 19 now but it's soon to be $21 trillion. But we defend everybody. When in doubt, come to the United States. We'll defend you. In some cases

---

[231] *Id.* at 81-83.
[232] Haberman & Sanger, *supra* note 223.

free of charge. And in all cases for a substantially, you know, greater amount. We spend a substantially greater amount than what the people are paying.[233]

That same month, candidate Trump spoke to CBS News about U.S. spending to NATO. He said then:

> NATO was set up when we were a richer country. We're not a rich country anymore. We're borrowing, we're borrowing all of this money . . . NATO is costing us a fortune and yes, we're protecting Europe with NATO but we're spending a lot of money. Number one, I think the distribution of costs has to be changed.[234]

As president, President Trump has continued to press European allies to contribute more NATO defense. For example, in a tweet on July 9, 2018, President Trump wrote:

> The United States is spending far more on NATO than any other Country. This is not fair, nor is it acceptable. While these countries have been increasing their contributions since I took office, they must do much more. Germany is at 1%, the U.S. is at 4%, and NATO benefits.......[235]

Jens Stoltenberg, the NATO Secretary-General, acknowledged in an interview that President Trump's message has "helped" NATO member countries to increase defense spending, commending the President on "his strong message on burden sharing."[236]

NSC Senior Director Tim Morrison explained the President's specific views about burden sharing regarding Ukraine during his public testimony. He testified:

> Q. And the President was also interested, was he not, in better understanding opportunities for increased burden sharing among the Europeans?
>
> A. Yes.
>
> Q. And what can you tell us about that?
>
> A. The President was concerned that the United States seemed to – to bear the exclusive brunt of security assistance to Ukraine. He wanted to see the Europeans step up and contribute more security assistance.

---

[233] *Id.*

[234] Shayna Freisleben, *A Guide to Trump's Past Comments about NATO*, CBS News, (Apr. 12, 2017).

[235] Donald J. Trump (@realDonaldTrump), Twitter (Jul. 9, 2018, 7:55 a m.), https://twitter.com/realDonaldTrump/status/1016289620596789248.

[236] David Greene, *After Trump's NATO Criticism, Countries Spend More on Defense*, NPR.org, (May 18, 2018).

Q. And was there any interagency activity, whether it be with the State Department for or the Defense Department, in coordination by the National Security Council, to look into that a little bit for the President?

A. We were surveying the data to understand who was contributing what and sort of in what categories.

Q. And so the President's evinced concerns, the interagency tried to address them?

A. Yes.[237]

In his public testimony, LTC Vindman confirmed the President's concerns about U.S. allies sharing the burden for mutual defense.[238]

3. U.S. foreign aid is often conditioned or paused, and U.S. security assistance to Ukraine has been paused before.

U.S. taxpayer-funded assistance to foreign governments is not an entitlement. The United States often conditions foreign aid on actions by recipient nations. In addition, foreign aid can, and often does, get delayed for various reasons. The pause of U.S. security assistance to Ukraine in this case is therefore not presumptive evidence of misconduct.

The United States conditions foreign assistance to a number of nations as a result of concerns about corruption, human rights abuses, or other issues. On October 31, 2019, the Trump Administration announced that it would withhold $105 million in security assistance for Lebanon shortly after the resignation of Lebanese Prime Minister Saad al-Hariri.[239] In September 2019, the State Department announced that it was withholding $160 million in aid from Afghanistan, citing corruption.[240] In June 2019, the Administration told Congress that it would reallocate $370 million in aid to Central American nations and suspend an additional $180 million in an effort to incentivize those countries to reduce the number of migrants reaching the U.S. border.[241] In 2017, President Trump froze $195 million in security assistance to Egypt—one of the largest recipients of U.S. aid—due to frustration with the country's poor track record on human rights and a recently enacted law regarding nongovernmental organizations.[242]

---

[237] *Impeachment Inquiry: Ambassador Kurt Volker and Mr. Timothy Morrison, supra* note 8.

[238] *Impeachment Inquiry: LTC Alexander Vindman and Ms. Jennifer Williams, supra* note 6.

[239] Patricia Zengerle & Mike Stone, *Exclusive: U.S. withholding $105 million in security aid for Lebanon- sources,* Reuters, Oct. 31, 2019.

[240] Tal Axelrod, *US withholds $160M in Afghan aid citing corruption,* The Hill, Sept. 9, 2019.

[241] Lesley Wroughton & Patricia Zengerle, *As promised, Trump slashes aid to Central America over migrants,* Reuters, Jun. 17, 2019.

[242] Gardiner Harris & Declan Walsh, *U.S. Slaps Egypt on Human Rights Record and Ties to North Korea,* N.Y. Times, Aug. 22, 2017.

The Democrats' witnesses explained that it is not unusual for foreign aid to be paused or even withheld. Ambassador Taylor testified that U.S. aid to foreign countries can be paused in various instances, such as a Congressional hold.[243] Ambassador Volker testified that foreign assistance can be delayed for a multitude of reasons and that "this hold on security assistance [to Ukraine] was not significant."[244] Ambassador Volker elaborated during his public testimony:

> Q. Ambassador Volker, you testified during your deposition that aid, in fact, does get held up from time-to-time for a whole assortment of reasons. Is that your understanding?
>
> A. That is true.
>
> Q. And sometimes the holdups are rooted in something at OMB, sometimes it's at the Defense Department, sometimes it's at the State Department, sometimes it's on the Hill. Is that correct?
>
> A. That is correct.
>
> Q. And so, when the aid was held up for 55 days for Ukraine, that didn't in and of itself strike you as uncommon?
>
> A. No. It's something that had happened in my career in the past. I had seen holdups of assistance. I just assumed it was part of the decision-making process. Somebody had an objection, and we had to overcome it.[245]

Ambassador David Hale, the Under Secretary of State for Political Affairs, agreed that U.S. taxpayer-funded aid has been paused from several countries around the world for various reasons and, in some cases, for unknown reasons.[246] Ambassador Hale elaborated:

> We've often heard at the State Department that the President of the United States wants to make sure that foreign assistance is reviewed scrupulously to make sure that it's truly in U.S. national interests, and that we evaluate it continuously, so that it meets certain criteria that the President has established.[247]

Ambassador Hale explained that the NSC launched a review of U.S. foreign assistance to ensure U.S. taxpayer money was spent efficiently and to advance "[t]he principle of burden sharing by allies and other like-minded states."[248] Dr. Hill, the NSC's Senior Director for Europe, testified that as she was leaving NSC in July 2019, "there had been more scrutiny" to assistance:

---

[243] Taylor deposition, *supra* note 47, at 170-71.

[244] Volker transcribed interview, *supra* note 60, at 78-80.

[245] *Impeachment Inquiry: Ambassador Kurt Volker and Mr. Timothy Morrison, supra* note 8.

[246] *"Impeachment Inquiry: Ms. Laura Cooper and Mr. David Hale": Hearing before the H. Perm. Sel. Comm. on Intelligence*, 116th Cong. (2019).

[247] *Id.*

[248] *Id.*

As I understood them, there had been a directive for whole-scale review of our foreign policy, foreign policy assistance, and the ties between our foreign policy objectives and the assistance. This had been going on actually for many months. And in the period when I was wrapping up my time there, there had been more scrutiny than specific assistance to specific sets of countries as a result of that overall view – review.[249]

The Democrats' witnesses also described how U.S. foreign assistance to Ukraine has been delayed in the past. Dr. Hill testified that security assistance to Ukraine has been paused before "at multiple junctures" during her time at NSC, even with bipartisan support for the assistance.[250] Dr. Hill testified:

Q. On the issue of the security assistance freeze, had assistance for Ukraine ever been held up before during your time at NSC?

A. Yes.

Q. For what – and when was that?

A. At multiple junctures. You know, it gets back to the question that [Republican staff] asked before. There's often a question raised about assistance, you know, a range of assistance –

Q. But for Ukraine specifically?

A. Yeah, that's correct.

Q. Okay. Even though there's been bipartisan support for the assistance?

A. Correct.[251]

Catherine Croft, a former NSC director, offered an example in her deposition, explaining that OMB paused the sale of Javelin missiles to Ukraine in November or December 2017.[252] This pause, too, was eventually lifted and Ukraine received the missiles.[253]

---

[249] *Impeachment Inquiry: Dr. Fiona Hill and Mr. David Holmes, supra* note 210.
[250] Hill deposition, *supra* note 12, at 304.
[251] *Id.* at 303-04.
[252] Croft deposition, *supra* note 60, at 67.
[253] *Id.* at 68.

4. Despite President Trump's skepticism, the Trump Administration's policies have shown greater commitment and support to Ukraine than those of the Obama Administration.

Several of the Democrats' witnesses testified that President Trump has taken a stronger stance in supporting Ukraine. Dr. Hill testified that President Trump's decision to support Ukraine with lethal defensive weapons was a more robust policy than under the Obama Administration.[254] Ambassador Taylor characterized President Trump's policy as a "substantial improvement."[255] Ambassador Yovanovitch agreed, testifying:

> And I actually felt that in the 3 years that I was there, partly because of my efforts, but also the interagency team, and President Trump's decision to provide lethal weapons to Ukraine, that our policy actually got stronger over the three last 3 years [*sic*].[256]

She added:

> Q. Can you testify to the difference [to] the changes in aid to Ukraine with the new administration starting in 2017? The different initiatives, you know, as far as providing lethal weapons and –
>
> A. Yeah. Well, I think that most of the assistance programs that we had, you know, continued, and due to the generosity of the Congress actually were increased. And so that was a really positive thing, I think, for Ukraine and for us. In terms of lethal assistance, we all felt *it was very significant that this administration made the decision to provide lethal weapons to Ukraine*.[257]

Ambassador Volker also explained how President Trump's policies of providing lethal defensive assistance to Ukraine have been "extremely helpful" in deterring Russian aggression in Ukraine.[258] He explained:

> So there has been U.S. assistance provided to Ukraine for some time, under the Bush administration, Obama administration, and now under the Trump administration. I was particularly interested in the security assistance and lethal defensive weapons. The reason for this is this was something that the Obama administration did not approve. They did not want to send lethal defensive arms to Ukraine.
>
> I fundamentally disagreed with that decision. It is not my – you know, I was just a private citizen, but that's my opinion. I thought

---

[254] Hill deposition, *supra* note 12, at 196.
[255] Taylor deposition, *supra* note 47, at 155.
[256] Yovanovitch deposition, *supra* note 115, at 140-41 (emphasis added).
[257] *Id.* at 144.
[258] Volker transcribed interview, *supra* note 60, at 87.

that this is a country that is defending itself against Russian aggression. They had their military largely destroyed by Russia in 2014 and '15 and needed the help. And humanitarian assistance is great, and nonlethal assistance, you know, MREs and blankets and all, that's fine, but if you're being attacked with mortars and artilleries and tanks, you need to be able to fight back.

The argument against this assistance being provided, the lethal defensive assistance, was that it would be provocative and could escalate the fighting with Russia. I had a fundamentally different view that if we did not provide it, it's an inducement to Russia to keep up the aggression, and there's no deterrence of Russia from trying to go further into Ukraine. So I believed it was important to help them rebuild their defensive capabilities and to deter Russia. It's also a symbol of U.S. support.

So I argued very strongly from the time I was appointed by Secretary Tillerson that the rationale for why we were not providing lethal defensive assistance to me doesn't hold water and that is a much stronger rationale that we should be doing it.

That eventually became administration policy. It took a while, but Secretary Tillerson, you know, he wanted to think it through, see how that would play out. How would the allies react to this? How would Russia react to this? How would the Ukrainians handle it? And we managed those issues. Secretary Mattis was very much in favor. And they met. I did not meet with the President about this, but they met with the President and the President approved it.[259]

5. **Although security assistance to Ukraine was paused in July 2019, several witnesses testified that U.S. security assistance was not linked to any Ukrainian action on investigations.**

Several witnesses testified that U.S. security assistance was not linked to or conditioned on any Ukrainian action to investigate President Trump's political rival. Even after U.S. officials learned in early- to mid-July that the security assistance had been paused for unknown reasons, evidence suggests that there was not a link between U.S. security assistance and Ukrainian action to investigate President Trump's political rival.

LTC Vindman testified that he learned about a pause on security assistance on July 3.[260] Morrison said he learned of the pause around July 15.[261] According to Ambassador Taylor, he learned via conference call on July 18 that OMB had paused the security assistance to

---

[259] *Id.* at 84-86.
[260] Vindman deposition, *supra* note 12, at 178.
[261] Morrison deposition, *supra* note 12, at 16.

Ukraine.[262] Ambassador Taylor relayed that according to the OMB representative on the call, the pause was done at the direction of the President and the chief of staff.[263] Although a reason was not provided for the pause at the time, OMB official Mark Sandy testified that he learned in early September 2019 that the pause was related "to the President's concern about other countries contributing more to Ukraine."[264]

Despite the pause, testimony from the Democrats' witnesses suggests the assistance was not linked to Ukraine investigating President Trump's political rival. Ambassador Volker, the key intermediary between the Ukrainian government and U.S. officials, testified that he was aware of no *quid pro quo* and that the Ukrainian government never raised concerns to him about a *quid pro quo*.[265] He said that when Ambassador Taylor raised questions about the appearance of a *quid pro quo*, "I discussed with him that there is no linkage here. I view this as an internal thing, and we are going to get it fixed."[266] Ambassador Volker further explained that even if Ukrainians perceived the aid was linked to investigations, they "never raised" that possibility with him.[267] Ambassador Volker believed that given the trust he had developed with the Ukrainian government, the Ukrainians would have come to him with concerns about the security assistance.[268]

House Intelligence Committee Chairman Adam Schiff attempted to get Ambassador Volker to testify in his closed-door deposition that the Ukrainian government would have felt pressure to investigate President Trump's political rival once they learned that the security assistance was delayed.[269] Ambassador Volker refused to accept Chairman Schiff's conclusion. He testified:

> Q. The request is made. And even though the suspension may have occurred earlier, the request is made to investigate the Bidens, and then Ukraine learns, for mysterious reasons, hundreds of millions in military support is being withheld. Do I have the chronology correct?
>
> A. Yes.
>
> Q. At the point they learned that, wouldn't that give them added urgency to meet the President's request on the Bidens?
>
> A. I don't know the answer to that. The –

---

[262] Taylor deposition, *supra* note 47, at 27.
[263] *Id.* at 28.
[264] Deposition of Mark Sandy, in Wash., D.C., at 42 (Nov. 16, 2019). Sandy testified that in early September, OMB received "requests for information on what additional countries were contributing to Ukraine." *Id.* at 44. OMB provided that information sometime in the first week of September. *Id.* at 82.
[265] Volker transcribed interview, *supra* note 60, at 170, 300-01.
[266] *Id.* at 130.
[267] *Id.* at 284.
[268] *Id.* at 300-01.
[269] *Id.* at 124-28.

Q. Ambassador –

A. When that – no –

Q. – as a career diplomat, you can't venture –

A. But, Congressman, this is why I'm trying to the say the context is different, because at the time they learned that, if we assume it's August 29th, they had just had a visit from the National Security Advisor, John Bolton. That's a high level meeting already. He was recommending and working on scheduling the visit of President Zelensky to Washington. We were also working on a bilateral meeting to take place in Warsaw on the margins of a commemoration on the beginning of World War II. And in that context, I think the Ukrainians felt like things are going the right direction, and they had not done anything on – they had not done anything on an investigation, they had not done anything on a statement, and things were ramping up in terms of their engagement with the administration. So I think they were actually feeling pretty good by then.

Q. Ambassador, I find it remarkable as a career diplomat that you have difficulty acknowledging that when Ukraine learned that their aid had been suspended for unknown reasons, that this wouldn't add additional urgency to a request by the President of the United States. I find that remarkable.[270]

During his public testimony, in an exchange with Rep. Mike Turner, Ambassador Volker reiterated that there was no linkage between U.S. security assistance and investigations. He testified:

Q. Did the President of the United States ever say to you that he was not going to allow aid from the United States to go to the Ukraine unless there were investigations into Burisma, the Bidens, or the 2016 elections?

A. No, he did not.

Q. Did the Ukrainians ever tell you that they understood that they would not get a meeting with the President of the United States, a phone call with the President of the United States, military aid or foreign aid from the United States unless they undertook investigations of Burisma, the Bidens, or the 2016 elections?

A. No, they did not.

---

[270] *Id.* at 126-28 (question and answer with Chairman Adam Schiff).

Q. So I would assume, then, that the Ukrainians never told you that [Mayor] Giuliani had told them that, in order to get a meeting with the President, a phone call with the President, military aid or foreign aid from the United States, that they would have to do these investigations.

A. No.[271]

Similarly, Deputy Assistant Secretary Kent testified in his closed-door deposition that he also did not "associate" the security assistance to investigations."[272] Kent relayed how Ambassador Taylor had told him that Ambassador Sondland was "pushing" President Zelensky to give an interview during the Yalta European Strategy (YES) conference in Kyiv in mid-September.[273] Ambassador Taylor told Kent that the "hope" was if President Zelensky gave a public signal on investigations, the security assistance pause would lift; however, Ambassador Taylor asserted that "both Tim Morrison and Gordon Sondland said that they did not believe the two issues were linked."[274]

During his sworn deposition, Ambassador Sondland testified that he could not recall "any discussions with the White House about withholding U.S. security assistance from Ukraine in exchange for assistance with President Trump's 2020 election campaign."[275] Ambassador Sondland testified that he was "never" aware of any preconditions on the delay of security assistance to Ukraine, or that the aid was tied to Ukraine undertaking any investigations.[276]

Although media reports allege that Ambassador Sondland later recanted this testimony to "confirm" a *quid pro quo*,[277] those reports exaggerate the supplemental information that Ambassador Sondland later provided. In a written supplement to his deposition testimony, Ambassador Sondland asserted that by the beginning of September 2019, "in the absence of any credible explanation for the suspension of aid, [he] **presumed** that the aid suspension had become linked to the proposed anti-corruption statement."[278] Ambassador Sondland asserted that he spoke to Yermak in Warsaw on September 1 and conveyed that U.S. aid would not "likely" flow until Ukraine provided an anti-corruption statement.[279] Yermak, however, in an interview with *Bloomberg*, disputed Ambassador Sondland's account, saying that he "bumped into" Ambassador Sondland and "doesn't remember any reference to military aid."[280]

---

[271] *Impeachment Inquiry: Ambassador Kurt Volker and Mr. Timothy Morrison, supra* note 8.

[272] Kent deposition, *supra* note 65, at 323.

[273] *Id.* at 269.

[274] *Id.*; *see also id.* at 323.

[275] Sondland deposition, *supra* note 51, at 35.

[276] *Id.* at 197.

[277] *See, e.g.*, Andrew Desiderio & Kyle Cheney, *Sondland reverses himself on Ukraine, confirming quid pro quo*, Politico, Nov. 5, 2019.

[278] Declaration of Ambassador Gordon D. Sondland at ¶ 4 (Nov. 4, 2019) (emphasis added) [hereinafter "Sondland declaration"].

[279] *Id.* at ¶ 5.

[280] Stephanie Baker & Daryna Krasnolutska, *Ukraine's fraught summer included a rogue embassy in Washington*, Bloomberg, Nov. 22, 2019.

Ambassador Sondland's addendum does not prove a nefarious *quid pro quo*. At most, and even discounting Yermak's subsequent denial, the addendum shows that as of September 1, Ambassador Sondland assumed there was a connection and relayed this assumption to Yermak— an assumption that the President would later tell Ambassador Sondland was inaccurate.[281]

During his deposition, Ambassador Taylor testified that he spoke by phone with Ambassador Sondland on September 8.[282] Ambassador Taylor recounted how Ambassador Sondland told him that President Trump wanted President Zelensky to "clear things up and do it in public" but there was no "*quid pro quo*."[283]

On September 9, Ambassador Sondland texted Ambassador Volker and Ambassador Taylor: "The President has been crystal clear: no *quid pro quo*'s [*sic*] of any kind. The President is trying to evaluate whether Ukraine is truly going to adopt the transparency and reforms that President Zelensky promised during his campaign."[284] When asked about this text message during his transcribed interview, Ambassador Volker testified that "Gordon was repeating here what we all understood."[285]

In his public testimony, Ambassador Taylor clarified his statement from his closed-door deposition that he had "clear understanding" that Ukraine would not receive security assistance until President Zelensky committed to investigations.[286] He explained his "clear understanding" came from Ambassador Sondland, who acknowledged that he had *presumed* there to be a linkage. In an exchange with Rep. Jim Jordan, Ambassador Taylor testified:

> Q. So what I'm wondering is, where did you get this clear understanding?
>
> A. As I testified, Mr. Jordan, this came from Ambassador Sondland.
>
> ***
>
> Q. You said you got this from Ambassador Sondland.
>
> A. That is correct. Ambassador Sondland also said he had talked to President Zelensky and Mr. Yermak and had told them that, although this was not a *quid pro quo*, if President Zelensky did not clear things up in public, we would be at a stalemate. That was the – that was one point.
>
> ***

---

[281] *See infra* note 297 and accompanying text.
[282] Taylor deposition, *supra* note 47, at 39.
[283] *Id.*
[284] Text message from Gordon Sondland to William Taylor and Kurt Volker (Sept. 9, 2019, 5:19 a.m.) [KV00000053].
[285] Volker transcribed interview, *supra* note 60, at 170.
[286] *Impeachment Inquiry: Ambassador William B. Taylor and Mr. George Kent, supra* note 2.

Q. All right. So, again, just to recap, you had three meetings with President Zelensky; no linkage in those three meetings came up. Ambassador Zelensky didn't announce that he was going [to] do any investigation of the Bidens or Burisma before the aid was released. He didn't –

A. That was President –

Q. – do a tweet, didn't do anything on CNN, didn't do any of that. President Zelensky. Excuse me.

A. Yeah. Right.

Q. And then what you have in front of you is an addendum that Mr. Sondland made to his testimony that we got a couple weeks ago. It says, "Declaration of Ambassador Gordon Sondland. I, Gordon Sondland, do hereby swear and affirm as follows." I want to you look at point number two, bullet point number two, second sentence. "Ambassador Taylor recalls that Mr. Morrison told Ambassador Taylor that I told Mr. Morrison that I conveyed this message to Mr. Yermak on September 1st, 2019, in connection with Vice President Pence's visit to Warsaw and a meeting with President Zelensky." Now, this is his clarification. Let me read it one more time. "Ambassador Taylor recalls that Mr. Morrison told Ambassador Taylor that I told Mr. Morrison that I had conveyed this message to Mr. Yermak on September 1st, 2019, in connection with Vice President Pence's visit to Warsaw and a meeting with President Zelensky." We've got six people having four conversations in one sentence, and you just told me this is where you got your clear understanding, which – I mean, even though you had three opportunities with President Zelensky for him to tell you, "You know what? We're going to do these investigations to get the aid," he didn't tell you, three different times. Never makes an announcement, never tweets about it, never does the CNN interview. Ambassador, you weren't on the call, were you? The President – you didn't listen in on President Trump's call and President Zelensky's call?

A. I did not.

Q. You never talked with Chief of Staff Mulvaney.

A. I never did.

Q. You never met the President.

A. That's correct.

Q. You had three meetings again with Zelensky and it didn't come up.

A. And two of those, they had never heard about it, as far as I know, so there was no reason for it to come up.

Q. And President Zelensky never made an announcement. This is what I can't believe. And you're their star witness. You're their first witness.

A. Mr. Jordan –

Q. You're the guy. You're the guy based on this, based on – I mean, I've seen church prayer chains that are easier to understand than this.[287]

During his public testimony, Ambassador Sondland made clear that no one had ever told him that the security assistance was tied to Ukraine investigating the President's political rival. In particular, Ambassador Sondland explained that "President Trump never told me directly that the aid was conditioned on the meetings."[288] In an exchange with Rep. Turner, Ambassador Sondland elaborated:

Q. What about the aid? [Ambassador Volker] says that they weren't tied, that the aid was not tied—

A. And I didn't say they were conclusively tied either. I said I was presuming it.

Q. Okay. And so the President never told you they were tied.

A. That is correct.

Q. So your testimony and [Ambassador Volker's] testimony is consistent, and the President did not tie aid to investigations.

A. That is correct.

***

Q. So no one told you, not just the President. [Mayor] Giuliani didn't tell you. [Acting Chief of Staff] Mulvaney didn't tell you. Nobody—[Secretary] Pompeo didn't tell you. Nobody else on this planet told

[287] *Impeachment Inquiry: Ambassador William B. Taylor and Mr. George Kent, supra* note 2.
[288] *Impeachment inquiry: Ambassador Gordon Sondland, supra* note 56.

you that Donald Trump was tying aid to these investigations. Is that correct?

A. I think I already testified to that.

Q. No. Answer the question. Is it correct? No one on this planet told you that Donald Trump was tying aid to the investigations? Because if your answer is yes, then the chairman is wrong and the headline on CNN is wrong. No one on this planet told you that President Trump was tying aid to investigations, yes or no?

A. Yes.[289]

6. President Trump rejected any linkage between U.S. security assistance and Ukrainian action on investigations.

The evidence also shows that when President Trump was asked about a potential linkage between U.S. security assistance and Ukrainian investigations into the President's political rival, the President vehemently denied any connection. This evidence is persuasive because the President made the same denial twice to two separate senior U.S. officials in private, where there is no reason for the President to be anything less than completely candid.

In an interview with the *Wall Street Journal* and a detailed written submission to the impeachment inquiry, Senator Ron Johnson, the Chairman of the Senate Foreign Relations Subcommittee on Europe, disclosed that he spoke to President Trump on August 31, after learning from Ambassador Sondland that U.S. security assistance may be linked to Ukraine's willingness to demonstrate its commitment to fight corruption.[290] Senator Johnson explained that his purpose for calling President Trump was "to inform President Trump of my upcoming trip to Ukraine and to try to persuade him to authorize me to tell [President] Zelensky that the hold would be lifted on military aid."[291]

Senator Johnson recounted that President Trump was "not prepared" to lift the pause on security assistance to Ukraine, citing Ukrainian corruption and frustration that Europe did not share more of the burden.[292] Echoing his continual statements about U.S. allies sharing the financial burden for mutual defense, President Trump told Senator Johnson: "Ron, I talk to Angela [Merkel, German chancellor] and ask her, 'why don't you fund these things,' and she tells me, 'because we know you will.' We're schmucks, Ron. We're schmucks."[293]

When Senator Johnson raised the potential of a linkage between U.S. security assistance and investigations, President Trump vehemently denied it.[294] According to Senator Johnson,

---

[289] *Id.*

[290] Letter from Sen. Johnson, *supra* note 138, at 5; Siobhan Hughes & Rebecca Ballhaus, *Trump, in August call with GOP Senator, denied official's claim on Ukraine aid*, Wall St. J., Oct. 4, 2019.

[291] Letter from Sen. Johnson, *supra* note 138, at 5.

[292] *Id.*

[293] *Id.*

[294] *Id.*

Without hesitation, President Trump immediately denied such an arrangement existed. As reported in the *Wall Street Journal*, I quoted the President as saying, "[Expletive deleted]—No way. I would never do that. Who told you that?" ***I have accurately characterized his reaction as adamant, vehement and angry*** – there was more than one expletive that I have deleted.[295]

At the end of the phone call, President Trump circled back to Senator Johnson's request to release the pause on security assistance. President Trump said: "Ron, I understand your position. We're reviewing it now, and you'll probably like my final decision."[296] This conversation occurred on August 31, well before the Democrats initiated their impeachment inquiry, and undermines the assertion that the President fabricated legitimate reasons for the pause in security assistance in response to the Democrats' impeachment inquiry.

During his deposition, Ambassador Sondland testified that he called President Trump on September 9 and asked him "What do you want from Ukraine?" The President's response was "Nothing. There is no *quid pro quo*."[297] During his deposition, Ambassador Sondland testified:

> Q. So when you telephoned the President, tell us what happened.
>
> A. Well, from the time that the aid was help up until I telephoned the President there were a lot of rumors swirling around as to why the aid had been help up, including they wanted a review, they wanted Europe to do more. There were all kinds of rumors. And I know in my few previous conversations with the President he's not big on small talk to I would have one shot to ask him. And rather than asking him, "Are you doing X because of X or because of Y or because of Z?" ***I asked him one open-ended question: What do you want from Ukraine? And as I recall, he was in a very bad mood. It was a very quick conversation. He said: I wanted nothing. I want no quid pro quo. I want Zelensky to do the right thing. And I said: What does that mean? And he said: I want him to do what he ran on.***[298]

When asked about his conversation with Senator Johnson—which prompted Senator Johnson to call President Trump—Ambassador Sondland testified that he was "speculating" about the linkage between security assistance and investigations.[299] He explained:

> I noticed in the media [Senator Johnson] had come out and said that he and I had a conversation on the phone about it. And he had said

---

[295] *Id.* (emphasis added).
[296] *Id.*
[297] Sondland deposition, *supra* note 51, at 106.
[298] *Id.* at 105-06 (emphasis added).
[299] *Id.* at 196.

that I told him – this is in the media report, and I haven't discussed this with him since that media report – that I had said there was a *quid pro quo*. And I don't remember telling him that because I'm not sure I knew that at that point. I think what I might have done is I might have been speculating – I hope there's no, I hope this isn't being held up for nefarious reasons.[300]

Although Democrats and some in the media believe that Acting Chief of Staff Mick Mulvaney confirmed the existence of a *quid pro quo* during an October 2019 press briefing,[301] a careful reading of his statements shows otherwise. Chief of Staff Mulvaney cited President Trump's concerns about Ukrainian corruption and foreign aid in general as the "driving factors" in the temporary pause on security assistance.[302] He explained that Ukraine's actions in the 2016 election "was part of the thing that [the President] was worried about in corruption with that nation."[303] Chief of Staff Mulvaney specified, however, that "the money held up had absolutely nothing to do with [Vice President] Biden."[304]

7. Senior U.S. officials never substantively discussed the delay in security assistance with Ukrainian officials before the July 25 call.

Evidence also suggests that the senior levels of the Ukrainian government did not know that U.S. security assistance was delayed until some point after the July 25 phone call between President Trump and President Zelensky. Although the assistance was delayed at the time of the July 25 call, President Trump never raised the assistance with President Zelensky or implied that the aid was in danger. As Ambassador Volker testified, because Ukrainian officials were unaware of the pause on security assistance, "there was no leverage implied."[305] This evidence undercuts the allegation that the President withheld U.S. security assistance to pressure President Zelensky to investigate his political rival.

Most of the Democrats' witnesses, including Ambassador Taylor, traced their knowledge of the pause to a July 18 interagency conference call, during which OMB announced a pause on security assistance to Ukraine.[306] However, the two U.S. diplomats closest the Ukrainian government—Ambassador Volker and Ambassador Taylor—testified that Ukraine did not know about the delay "until the end of August," six weeks later, after it was reported publicly by *Politico* on August 28.[307]

---

[300] *Id.*

[301] *Impeachment Inquiry: Dr. Fiona Hill and Mr. David Holmes, supra* note 210 (statement of Rep. Adam Schiff, Chairman); Aaron Blake, *Trump's acting chief of staff admits it: There was a Ukraine quid pro quo*, Wash. Post, Oct. 17, 2019.

[302] The White House, Press Briefing by Acting Chief of Staff Mick Mulvaney (Oct. 17, 2019).

[303] *Id.*

[304] *Id.*

[305] Volker transcribed interview, *supra* note 60, at 124-25.

[306] *See, e.g.*, Taylor deposition, *supra* note 47, at 27.

[307] Volker transcribed interview, *supra* note 60, at 125, 266-67; Taylor deposition, *supra* note 47, at 119-20.

Ambassador Volker, the chief interlocutor with the Ukrainian government, testified that he never informed the Ukrainians about the delay.[308] The Ukrainian government only raised the issue with Ambassador Volker after reading about the delay in *Politico* in late August.[309] Explaining why the delay was not "significant, Ambassador Volker testified:

> Q. Looking back on it now, is [the delayed security assistance] something, in the grand scheme of things, that's very significant? I mean, is this worthy of investigating, or is this just another chapter in the rough and tumble world of diplomacy and foreign assistance?
>
> A. In my view, this hold on security assistance was not significant. I don't believe – in fact, I am quite sure that at least I, Secretary Pompeo, the official representatives of the U.S., never communicated to Ukrainians that it is being held for a reason. We never had a reason. And I tried to avoid talking to Ukrainians about it for as long as I could until it came out in *Politico* a month later because I was confident we were going to get it fixed internally.[310]

During his public testimony, Ambassador Volker confirmed that he did not have any communication with the Ukrainian government about the pause on U.S. security assistance until they raised the topic with him.[311] Morrison likewise testified that he avoided discussing the pause on security assistance with the Ukrainian government.[312]

Ambassador Taylor similarly testified that the Ukrainian government was not aware of the pause on U.S. security assistance until late August 2019. In an exchange with Rep. Ratcliffe, he explained:

> Q. So, based on your knowledge, nobody in the Ukrainian government became aware of a hold on military aid until 2 days later, on August 29th.
>
> A. That's my understanding.
>
> Q. That's your understanding. And that would have been well over a month after the July 25th call between President Trump and President Zelensky.
>
> A. Correct.
>
> Q. So you're not a lawyer, are you, Ambassador Taylor?

---

[308] Volker transcribed interview, *supra* note 60, at 80.

[309] *Id.* at 80-81; Text message from Andrey Yermak to Kurt Volker, (Aug. 29, 2019, 03:06:14 AM), [KV00000020]; *see* Caitlin Emma & Connor O'Brien, *Trump holds up Ukraine military aid meant to confront Russia*, Politico, Aug. 28, 2019.

[310] Volker transcribed interview, *supra* note 60, at 80.

[311] *Impeachment Inquiry: Ambassador Kurt Volker and Mr. Timothy Morrison, supra* note 8.

[312] *Id.*

A. I am not.

Q. Okay. So the idea of a *quid pro quo* is it's a concept where there is a demand for an action or an attempt to influence action in exchange for something else. And in this case, when people are talking about a *quid pro quo*, that something else is military aid. So, if nobody in the Ukrainian government is aware of a military hold at the time of the Trump-Zelensky call, then, as a matter of law and as a matter of fact, there can be no *quid pro quo* based on military aid. I just want to be real clear that, again, as of July 25th, you have no knowledge of a *quid pro quo* involving military aid.

A. July 25th is a week after the hold was put on the security assistance. And July 25th, they had a conversation between the two presidents where it was not discussed.

Q. And to your knowledge, nobody in the Ukrainian government was aware of the hold?

A. That is correct.[313]

Likewise, Philip Reeker, the Acting Assistant Secretary of State for Europeans Affairs, testified that he was unaware of any U.S. official conveying to a Ukrainian official that President Trump sought political investigations.[314] Acting Assistant Secretary Reeker testified that he was not aware of whether Ambassador Volker or Ambassador Sondland had such conversations with the Ukrainians.[315]

Some witnesses testified that the Ukrainian embassy made informal inquiries about the status of the security assistance. LTC Vindman recalled receiving "light queries" from his Ukrainian embassy counterparts about the aid in either early- or mid-August, but he was unable to pinpoint specific dates, or even the week, that he had such conversations.[316] LTC Vindman testified that Ukrainian questions about the delay were not "substantive" or "definitive" until around the time of the Warsaw summit, on September 1.[317] State Department official Catherine Croft testified that two individuals from the Ukrainian embassy approached her about a pause on security assistance at some point before August 28, but Croft told them she "was confident that any issues in process would get resolved."[318] Deputy Assistant Secretary of Defense Laura Cooper testified publicly that her staff received inquiries from the Ukrainian embassy in July that "there was some kind of issue" with the security assistance; however, she did not know what the Ukrainian government knew at the time.[319]

---

[313] Taylor deposition, *supra* note 47, at 119-20.
[314] Deposition of Philip Reeker in Wash., D.C., at 149 (Oct. 26, 2019).
[315] *Id.* at 150.
[316] Vindman deposition, *supra* note 12, at 135-37, 189-90.
[317] *Id.* at 189-90.
[318] Croft deposition, *supra* note 60, at 86-87.
[319] *Impeachment Inquiry: Ms. Laura Cooper and Mr. David Hale, supra* note 246.

Although this evidence suggests that Ukrainian officials in Washington were vaguely aware of an issue with the security assistance before August 28, the evidence does not show that the senior leadership of Ukrainian government in Kyiv was aware of the pause until late August. A *New York Times* story claimed that unidentified Ukrainian officials were aware of a delay in "early August" 2019 but said there was no stated link between that delay and any investigative demands.[320] However, a subsequent *Bloomberg* story reported that President Zelensky "and his key advisers learned of [the pause on U.S. security assistance] only in a *Politico* report in late August."[321]

The *Bloomberg* story detailed how Ukraine's embassy in Washington—led by then-Ambassador Chaly, who had been appointed by President Zelensky's predecessor—went "rogue" in the early months of the Zelensky administration.[322] According to Andrey Yermak, a close adviser to President Zelensky, the Ukrainian embassy officials, who were loyal to former President Poroshenko, did not inform President Zelensky that there was any issue with the U.S. security assistance.[323] This information explains the conflicting testimony between witnesses like LTC Vindman and Deputy Assistant Secretary Cooper, who testified that the Ukrainian embassy raised questions about the security assistance, and Ambassador Volker and Ambassador Taylor, who testified that the Zelensky government did not know about any pause in security assistance.

According to the Ukrainian government, President Zelensky and his senior advisers only learned of the pause on security assistance from *Politico*—severely undercutting the idea that President Trump was seeking to pressure Ukraine to investigate his political rival.

8. The Ukrainian government denied any awareness of a linkage between U.S. security assistance and investigations.

Publicly available information also shows clearly that the Ukrainian government leadership denied any awareness of a linkage between U.S. security assistance and investigations into the President's political rival. The Ukrainian government leaders made this assertion following public reports that Ambassador Sondland had raised the potential connection in early September. This understanding is supported by information provided by Senator Johnson.

In Ambassador Sondland's addendum to his closed-door testimony, dated November 5, 2019, he wrote how he came to perceive a connection between security assistance and the investigations. He wrote:

> [B]y the beginning of September 2019, and in the absence of any credible explanation for the suspension of aid, I presumed that the aid suspension had become linked to the proposed anti-corruption

---

[320] Andrew E. Kramer & Kenneth P. Vogel, *Ukraine knew of aid freeze by early August, undermining Trump defense*, N.Y. Times, Oct. 23, 2019.
[321] Baker & Krasnolutska, *supra* note 280.
[322] *Id.*
[323] *Id.*

statement. . . . And it would have been natural for me to have voiced what I had presumed to Ambassador Taylor, Senator Johnson, the Ukrainians, and Mr. Morrison.[324]

Following media reports of Ambassador Sondland's addendum, Ukrainian Foreign Minister Prystaiko told the media that Ambassador Sondland had not linked the security assistance to Ukrainian action on investigations.[325] He said: "Ambassador Sondland did not tell us, and certainly did not tell me, about a connection between the assistance and the investigations."[326] Minister Prystaiko went further to say that he was never aware of any connection between security assistance and investigations: "*I have never seen a direct relationship between investigations and security assistance.* Yes, the investigations were mentioned, you know, in the conversation of the presidents. But there was no clear connection between these events."[327]

Senator Johnson explained that he had three meetings with senior Ukrainian government officials in June and July 2019.[328] Two of meetings were with Oleksandr Danylyuk, then-secretary of Ukraine's National Security and Defense Council, and Valeriy Chaly, then-Ukrainian Ambassador to the U.S.[329] Senator Johnson said that none of the these Ukrainian officials raised any concerns with him about security assistance or investigations: "At no time during those meetings did anyone from Ukraine raise the issue of the withholding of military aid or express concerns regarding pressure being applied by the president or his administration."[330]

9. The Ukrainian government considered issuing a public anti-corruption statement to convey that President Zelensky was "serious and different" from previous Ukrainian regimes.

Evidence shows that in light of President Trump's deep-rooted skepticism about Ukraine, and working in tandem with senior U.S. officials, the Ukrainian government sought to convince President Trump that the new regime took corruption seriously. This commitment took two potential forms: a public statement that Ukraine would investigate corruption or a media interview about investigations. Although the parties later discussed the inclusion of specific investigations proposed by Mayor Giuliani, U.S. officials explained that the intent of the statement was to convey a public commitment to anti-corruption reform and that they did not associate the statement with an investigation of the President's political rival.

Ambassador Volker explained the goal of having Ukraine convey President Zelensky's commitment to reform and fighting corruption in a public message. He testified:

A. So the issue as I understood it was this deep-rooted, skeptical view of Ukraine, a negative view of Ukraine, preexisting 2019, you know,

---

[324] Sondland declaration, *supra* note 278, at ¶4.

[325] *U.S. envoy Sondland did not link Biden probe to aid: Ukraine minister*, Reuters, Nov. 14, 2019.

[326] *Id.*

[327] *Id.* (emphasis added).

[328] Letter from Sen. Ron Johnson, *supra* note 138, at 4.

[329] *Id.*

[330] *Id.* at 4-5.

going back. When I started this I had one other meeting with President Trump and President Poroshenko. It was in September of 2017. And at that time he had a very skeptical view of Ukraine. So I know he had a very deep-rooted skeptical view. And my understanding at the time was that even though he agreed in the [May 23] meeting that we had with him, say, okay, I'll invite him, he didn't really want to do it. And that's why the meeting kept being delayed and delayed. And we ended up at a point in talking with the Ukrainians – who we'll come to this, but, you know, who had asked to communicate with Giuliani – that they wanted to convey that they really are different. And we ended up talking about, well, then, make a statement about investigating corruption and your commitment to reform and so forth.

Q. Is that the statement that you discussed in your text messages –

A. Yes.

Q. – around August of 2019?

A. Yes.

Q. Okay.

A. Yeah. To say make a statement along those lines. And *the thought behind that was just trying to be convincing that they are serious and different from the Ukraine of the past.*[331]

Ambassador Volker elaborated during his public testimony that a public statement is not unusual. He explained:

> I didn't find it that unusual. I think when you're dealing with a situation where I believe the President was highly skeptical about President Zelensky being committed to really changing Ukraine after his entirely negative view of the country, that he would want to hear something more from President Zelensky to be convinced that, "Okay, I'll give this guy a chance."[332]

The Democrats' witnesses explained how the idea of a public statement arose. Ambassador Volker testified that Andrey Yermak, a senior adviser to President Zelensky, sent him a draft statement following Yermak's meeting with Mayor Giuliani on August 2.[333] Ambassador Volker said that he believed the statement was "valuable for getting the Ukrainian

---

[331] Volker transcribed interview, *supra* note 60, at 41-42 (emphasis added).
[332] *Impeachment Inquiry: Ambassador Kurt Volker and Mr. Timothy Morrison, supra* note 8.
[333] Volker transcribed interview, *supra* note 60, at 71.

Government on the record about their commitment to reform and change and fighting corruption because I believed that would be helpful in overcoming this deep skepticism that the President had about Ukraine."[334] Ambassador Volker, however, did not see the statement as a "necessary condition" for President Zelensky securing a White House meeting.[335]

Ambassador Volker explained that although the statement evolved to include specific references to "Burisma" and "2016," the goal was still to show that President Zelensky was "different." He testified:

> Q. And the draft statement went through some iterations. Is that correct?
>
> A Yeah. It was pretty quick, though. I don't know the timeline exactly. We have it. But, basically, Andrey [Yermak] sends me a text. I share it with Gordon Sondland. We have a conversation with Rudy to say: The Ukrainians are looking at this text. Rudy says: Well, if it doesn't say Burisma and if it doesn't say 2016, what does it mean? You know, it's not credible. You know, they're hiding something. And so we talked and I said: So what you're saying is just at the end of the – same statement, just insert Burisma and 2016, you think that would be more credible? And he said: Yes. So I sent that back to Andrey, conveyed the conversation with him – because he had spoken with Rudy prior to that, not me – conveyed the conversation, and Andrey said that he was not – he did not think this was a good idea, and I shared his view.
>
> Q. You had testified from the beginning you didn't think it was a good idea to mention Burisma or 2016.
>
> A. Correct.
>
> Q. But then, as I understand it, you came to believe that if we're going to do the statement, maybe it's necessary to have that reference in there, correct?
>
> A. I'd say I was in the middle. I wouldn't say I thought it was necessary to have it in there because I thought the target here is not the specific investigations. The target is getting Ukraine to be seen as credible in changing the country, fighting corruption, introducing reform, that Zelensky is the real deal. You may remember that there was a statement that Rudy Giuliani made when he canceled his visit to Ukraine in May of 2019 that President Zelensky is surrounded by enemies of the United States. And I just knew that to be

---

[334] *Id.*
[335] *Impeachment Inquiry: Ambassador Kurt Volker and Mr. Timothy Morrison, supra* note 8

fundamentally not true. And so I think, when you talk about overcoming skepticism, that's kind of what I'm talking about, getting these guys out there publicly saying: We are different.[336]

Although subsequent reporting has connoted a connection between "Burisma" and the Bidens,[337] the Democrats' witnesses testified that they did not have that understanding while working with the Ukrainian government about a potential statement. Ambassador Volker explained that "there is an important distinction about Burisma" and that Vice President Biden or Hunter Biden were "never part of the conversation" with the Ukrainians.[338] He also testified that the Ukrainians did not link Burisma to the Bidens: "They never mentioned Biden to me."[339] Ambassador Volker also made clear that following his initial conversation with Mayor Giuliani in May 2019, Mayor Giuliani "never brought up Biden or Bidens with me again. And so when we talked or heard Burisma, I literally meant Burisma and that, not the conflation of that with the Bidens."[340]

Ambassador Sondland testified that he was unaware that "Burisma" may have meant "Biden" until the White House released the July 25th call transcript on September 25.[341] In fact, Ambassador Sondland testified that he recalled no discussions with any State Department or White House official about former Vice President Joe Biden or Hunter Biden.[342] Ambassador Sondland testified that he did not recall Mayor Giuliani ever discussing the Bidens with him.[343]

Testimony and text messages reflect that Ambassador Volker, Ambassador Sondland, and Ambassador Taylor communicated about Ukraine's commitment to fight corruption throughout the summer. Ambassador Taylor testified that in a phone conversation on June 27, Ambassador Sondland told him that President Zelensky "needed to make clear to President Trump that he, President Zelensky, was not standing in the way of 'investigations.'"[344] Ambassador Taylor said he did not know to what "investigations" Ambassador Sondland was referring, but that Ambassador Volker "intended to pass that message [to President Zelensky] in Toronto several days later."[345]

In early July, Ambassador Volker explained the dynamic directly to President Zelensky in Toronto, emphasizing the need to demonstrate a commitment to reform. Ambassador Volker testified:

---

[336] Volker transcribed interview, *supra* note 60, at 71-73.

[337] *See, e.g.*, Paul Sonne, Michael Kranish, & Matt Viser, *The gas tycoon and the vice president's son: The story of Hunter Biden's foray into Ukraine,* Wash. Post, Sept. 28, 2019.

[338] Volker transcribed interview, *supra* note 60, at 73.

[339] *Id.* at 193.

[340] *Id.* at 213.

[341] Sondland deposition, *supra* note 51, at 70.

[342] *Id.* at 33. Ambassador Sondland testified that Burisma was "one of many examples" of Ukrainian corruption. *Id.* Ambassador Sondland mentioned Naftogaz as another example of Ukrainian corruption and lack of transparency that "[came] up at every conversation." *Id.* at 71, 99.

[343] *Id.* at 33.

[344] Taylor deposition, *supra* note 47, at 25.

[345] *Id.* at 62-65.

I believe [Mayor Giuliani] was getting bad information, and I believe that his negative messaging about Ukraine would be reinforcing the President's already negative position about Ukraine. So I discussed this with President Zelensky when I saw him in Toronto on July 3rd, and I said I think this is a problem that we have Mayor Giuliani – so I didn't discuss his meeting with Lutsenko then. That came later. I only learned about that later. But I discussed even on July 3rd with President Zelensky that you have a problem with your message of being, you know, clean, reform, that we need to support you, is not getting – or is getting countermanded or contradicted by a negative narrative about Ukraine, that it is still corrupt, there's still terrible people around you. At this time, there was concern about his chief of presidential administration, Andriy Bohdan, who had been a lawyer for a very famous oligarch in Ukraine. And so I discussed this negative narrative about Ukraine that Mr. Giuliani seemed to be furthering with the President.[346]

On July 21, Ambassador Sondland sent a text message to Ambassador Taylor that read: "[W]e need to get the conversation started and the relationship built, irrespective of the pretext. I am worried about the alternative."[347] Ambassador Sondland testified that the word "pretext" concerned agreement on an interview or press statement and that the "alternative" was no engagement at all between President Trump and President Zelensky.[348] Ambassador Sondland testified that he viewed giving a press interview or making a press statement as different from pressuring Ukraine to investigate political rival.[349]

On August 9, Ambassador Sondland sent a text message to Ambassador Volker, writing in part: "I think potus [sic] really wants the deliverable."[350] Ambassador Sondland testified that "deliverable" referred to the Ukrainian press statement.[351] Ambassador Volker testified that President Trump wanted a public commitment to reform as a "deliverable":

Q. And what – yeah, what did you understand what the President wanted by deliverable?

A. That statement that had been under conversation.

Q. That was the deliverable from Zelensky that the President wanted before he would commit to –

---

[346] Volker transcribed interview, *supra* note 60, at 137.
[347] Text message from Gordon Sondland to Kurt Volker & William Taylor (July 21, 2019, 4:45 a.m.) [KV00000037].
[348] Sondland deposition, *supra* note 51, at 183-84.
[349] *Id.* at 170-71.
[350] Text message from Gordon Sondland to Kurt Volker (Aug. 9, 2019, 5:47 p.m.) [KV00000042].
[351] Sondland deposition, *supra* note 51, at 290.

A. *He wanted to see that they're going to come out publicly and commit to reform, investigate the past*, et cetera.[352]

According to Ambassador Taylor, on September 8, Ambassador Sondland relayed to Ambassador Taylor that he had told President Zelensky and Yermak that if President Zelensky "did not clear things up in public, we would be at a stalemate."[353] Ambassador Taylor interpreted Ambassador Sondland's use of "stalemate" to mean that there would be no security assistance to Ukraine.[354] Ambassador Taylor recounted that Ambassador Sondland said that President Trump is a businessman and businessmen ask for something before "signing a check."[355] Ambassador Taylor testified that he understood that "signing a check" related to security assistance.[356] Ambassador Sondland did not recall the conversation with Ambassador Taylor and denied making a statement about President Trump seeking something for signing a check to Ukraine.[357] He testified:

> Q. So you hadn't – did you ever, in the course of this, ever make a statement to the effect of, you know, we're cutting a big check to the Ukraine, you know, what should we get for his?
>
> A. That's not something I would have said. I don't remember that at all.
>
> Q. Okay. So you've never made a statement relating the aid to conditions that the Ukrainians ought to comply with?
>
> A. I don't remember that, no.
>
> Q. But if someone suggested that you made that statement, that would be out of your own character, you're saying?
>
> A. Yes.[358]

Although Ambassador Sondland's statements imply that the President personally sought a conditionality on the security assistance, other witnesses testified that Ambassador Sondland had a habit of exaggerating his interactions with President Trump.[359] Ambassador Sondland himself acknowledged that he only spoke with the President five or six times, one of which was a Christmas greeting.[360] It is not readily apparent that Ambassador Sondland was speaking on behalf of President Trump in this context.

---

[352] Volker transcribed interview, *supra* note 60, at 184 (emphasis added).
[353] Taylor deposition, *supra* note 47, at 39.
[354] *Id.*
[355] *Id.* at 40
[356] *Id.*
[357] Sondland deposition, *supra* note 51, at 198-99, 351.
[358] *Id.* at 198-99.
[359] Hill deposition, *supra* note 12, at 240-41; Kent deposition, *supra* note 65, at 257.
[360] Sondland deposition, *supra* note 51, at 56.

10. President Zelensky never raised a linkage between security assistance and investigations in his meetings with senior U.S. government officials.

Between July 18—the date on which OMB announced the pause on security assistance to Ukraine during an interagency conference call—and September 11—when the pause was lifted—President Zelensky had five separate meetings with high-ranking U.S. government officials. The evidence shows that President Zelensky never raised any concerns in those meeting that he felt pressure to investigate President Trump's political rival or that U.S. security assistance to Ukraine was conditioned on any such investigations.

On July 25, President Zelensky spoke by telephone with President Trump. Although President Zelensky noted a desire to purchase additional Javelin missiles from the United States—an expenditure separate from security assistance—the call summary otherwise does not show that the President discussed a pause on U.S. security assistance to Ukraine.[361]

On July 26, President Zelensky met in Kyiv with Ambassador Volker, Ambassador Taylor, and Ambassador Sondland.[362] According to Ambassador Sondland's closed-door deposition, President Zelensky did not raise any concern about a pause on security assistance or a linkage between the aid and investigations into President Trump's political rival.[363]

On August 27, President Zelensky met in Kyiv with President Trump's then-National Security Advisor John Bolton.[364] According to Ambassador Taylor, President Zelensky and Ambassador Bolton did not discuss U.S. security assistance.[365]

On September 1, President Zelensky met in Warsaw with Vice President Pence, after the existence of the security assistance pause became public. Tim Morrison, Senior Director at the NSC, testified that President Zelensky raised the security assistance directly with Vice President Pence during their meeting.[366] According to Morrison, Vice President Pence relayed President Trump's concern about corruption, the need for reform in Ukraine, and his desire for other countries to contribute more to Ukrainian defense.[367] As Jennifer Williams, senior adviser for Europe in the Office of the Vice President, testified:

> Once the cameras left the room, the very first question that President Zelensky had was about the status of security assistance. And the VP responded by really expressing our ongoing support for Ukraine, but wanting to hear from President Zelensky, you know, what the status of his reform efforts were that he could then convey back to

---

[361] *Memorandum of Telephone Conversation, supra* note 15.
[362] Taylor deposition, *supra* note 47, at 31; Sondland deposition, *supra* note 51, at 29.
[363] Sondland deposition, *supra* note 51, at 252.
[364] Taylor deposition, *supra* note 47, at 33.
[365] *Id.*
[366] Morrison deposition, *supra* note 12, at 131-34.
[367] *Id.*

the President, and also wanting to hear if there was more that European countries could do to support Ukraine.[368]

Vice President Pence did not discuss any investigations with President Zelensky.[369] Morrison said that Vice President Pence spoke to President Trump that evening, who was "still skeptical" due to the fact that U.S. allies were not adequately contributing to Ukraine.[370] Although Ambassador Sondland claimed in his public hearing that he informed Vice President Pence of his assumption of a link between security assistance and investigations in advance of the Vice President's meeting with President Zelensky,[371] the Vice President's office said Ambassador Sondland never raised investigations or conditionality on the security assistance.[372]

On September 5, President Zelensky met in Kyiv with Senator Ron Johnson, Senator Chris Murphy, and Ambassador Taylor.[373] President Zelensky raised the issue of the security assistance, and Senator Johnson relayed to him what President Trump had told Senator Johnson during their August 31 conversation.[374] Senator Murphy then warned President Zelensky "not to respond to requests from American political actors or he would risk losing Ukraine's bipartisan support."[375] Senator Johnson recalled that he did not comment on Senator Murphy's statement but began discussing a potential presidential meeting.[376] To help President Zelensky understand President Trump's mindset, Senator Johnson "tried to portray [President Trump's] strongly held attitude and reiterated the reasons President Trump consistently gave [Senator Johnson] for his reservations regarding Ukraine: endemic corruption and inadequate European support."[377] Senator Johnson recounted how President Zelensky raised no concerns about pressure:

> This was a very open, frank, and supportive discussion. There was no reason for anyone on either side not to be completely honest or to withhold any concerns. *At no time during this meeting—or any other meeting on this trip—was there any mention by [President] Zelensky or any Ukrainian that they were feeling pressure to do anything in return for military aid*, not even after [Senator] Murphy warned them about getting involved in the 2020 election—which would have been the perfect time to discuss any pressure.[378]

---

[368] Williams deposition, *supra* note 73, at 81.

[369] *Impeachment Inquiry: Ambassador Kurt Volker and Mr. Timothy Morrison*, *supra* note 8; *Impeachment Inquiry: LTC Alexander Vindman and Ms. Jennifer Williams*, *supra* note 6. In fact, Williams testified that Vice President Pence has "never brought up" these investigations. *Impeachment Inquiry: LTC Alexander Vindman and Ms. Jennifer Williams*, *supra* note 6.

[370] Morrison deposition, *supra* note 12, at 133-34.

[371] *Impeachment Inquiry: Ambassador Gordon Sondland*, *supra* note 56.

[372] Office of the Vice President, Statement from VP Chief of Staff Marc Short (Nov. 20, 2019). In addition, the summary of President Trump's July 25 call with President Zelensky was not included in Vice President Pence's briefing book for his meeting with President Zelensky. Williams deposition, *supra* note 73, at 108.

[373] Sen. Johnson letter, *supra* note 138, at 6.

[374] *Id.*

[375] *Id.* at 7.

[376] *Id.*

[377] *Id.*

[378] *Id.* at 8 (emphasis added).

After Senator Johnson offered his perspective, Senator Murphy similarly provided an account of the September 5 meeting.[379] Senator Murphy did not dispute the facts as recounted by Senator Johnson, including that President Zelensky raised no concerns about feeling pressure to investigate the President's political rival.[380] Senator Murphy, however, interpreted President Zelensky's silence to mean that he felt pressure.[381] This "interpretation"—based on what President Zelensky did not say—is unpersuasive in light of President Zelensky's repeated and consistent statements that he felt no pressure.[382]

11. In early September 2019, President Zelensky's government implemented several anti-corruption reform measures.

Publicly available information shows that following the seating of Ukraine's new parliament, the Verkhovna Rada (Rada), on August 29, 2019, the Zelensky government initiated aggressive anti-corruption reforms. Almost immediately, President Zelensky appointed a new prosecutor general and opened Ukraine's Supreme Anti-Corruption Court.[383] On September 3, the Rada passed a bill that removed parliamentary immunity.[384] President Zelensky signed the bill on September 11.[385] On September 18, the Rada approved a bill streamlining corruption prosecutions and allowing the Supreme Anti-Corruption Court to focus on high-level corruption cases.[386]

Witnesses described how these legislative initiatives instilled confidence that Ukraine was delivering on anti-corruption reform. NSC staffer LTC Vindman testified that the Rada's efforts were significant.[387] In his deposition, Ambassador Taylor lauded President Zelensky for this demonstrable commitment to reform. He testified:

> President Zelensky was taking over Ukraine in a hurry. He had appointed reformist ministers and supported long-stalled anticorruption legislation. He took quick executive action, including opening Ukraine's High Anti-Corruption Court, which was established under previous Presidential administration but was never allowed to operate. . . . With his new parliamentary majority, President Zelensky changed the Ukrainian constitution to remove absolute immunity from Rada deputies, which had been the source of raw corruption for decades.[388]

---

[379] Letter from Sen. Chris Murphy to Adam Schiff, Chairman, H. Perm. Sel. Comm. on Intelligence, & Carolyn Maloney, Acting Chairwoman, H. Comm. on Oversight & Reform (Nov. 19, 2019).

[380] *Id.* at 5.

[381] *Id.*

[382] *See supra* Section I.A.2.

[383] Stefan Wolff & Tatyana Malyarenko, *In Ukraine, Volodymyr Zelenskiy must tread carefully or may end up facing another Maidan uprising*, The Conversation, Nov. 11, 2019.

[384] *Bill on lifting parliamentary immunity submitted to Zelensky for signature*, Unian, Sept. 4, 2019.

[385] *Zelensky signs law on stripping parliamentary immunity*, Interfax-Ukraine, Sept. 11, 2019.

[386] *Anti-corruption Court to receive cases from NABU, SAPO*, 112 UA, Sept. 18, 2019.

[387] *Impeachment Inquiry: LTC Alexander Vindman and Ms. Jennifer Williams, supra* note 6.

[388] Taylor deposition, *supra* note 47, at 22-23.

Likewise, NSC Senior Director Tim Morrison recalled that President Zelensky's team had literally been working through the night on anti-corruption reforms. He testified:

Q: And after the Rada was seated, do you know if President Zelensky made an effort to implement those [anti-corruption] reforms?

A: I do.

Q: And what reforms generally can you speak to?

A: Well, he named a new prosecutor general. That was something that we were specifically interested in. He had his party introduce a spate of legislative reforms, one of which was particularly significant was stripping Rada members of their parliamentary immunity. That passed fairly quickly, as I recall. Those kinds of things.

Q: And within what time period were some of those initial reforms passed?

A: Very, very quickly.

Q: Okay. So in the month of August?

A: When we were – when Ambassador Bolton was in Ukraine and he met with President Zelensky, we observed that everybody on the Ukrainian side of the table was exhausted, because they had been up for days working on, you know, reform legislation, working on the new Cabinet, to get through as much as possible on the first day.

Q: Remind me again of Ambassador Bolton's visit. Was that August, at the end of August?

A: It was at the end of August. It was between the G7 and the Warsaw commemoration

Q: So by Labor Day, for example?

A: I seem to recall we were – we – we were there on the opening day of the Rada. President – President Zelensky met with Ambassador Bolton on the opening day of the Rada, and they were in an all-night session. Yeah. So, I mean, things were happening that day.[389]

These actions by the Ukrainian government in early September 2019 are significant in demonstrating President Zelensky's commitment to fighting corruption. Although the

---

[389] Morrison deposition, *supra* note 12, at 128-29.

Department of Defense had certified Ukraine met its anti-corruption benchmarks in Spring 2019, that certification occurred before President Zelensky's inauguration.[390] Deputy Assistant Secretary of Defense Laura Cooper testified during her public hearing that the anti-corruption review examined the efforts of the Poroshenko administration and that President Zelensky had appointed a new Minister of Defense.[391]

As President Trump told Ambassador Sondland on September 9, he sought "nothing" from the Ukrainian government; he only wanted President Zelensky to "do what he ran on."[392] President Zelensky had run on an anti-corruption platform, and these early aggressive actions provided confirmation that he was the "real deal," as U.S. officials advised President Trump.

12. The security assistance was ultimately disbursed to Ukraine in September 2019 without any Ukrainian action to investigate President Trump's political rival.

On September 11, President Trump met with Vice President Pence, Senator Rob Portman, and Acting Chief of Staff Mick Mulvaney to discuss U.S. security assistance to Ukraine.[393] As recounted by NSC Senior Director Tim Morrison, the group discussed whether President Zelensky's progress on anti-corruption reform—which Vice President Pence discussed during his bilateral meeting with President Zelensky on September 1—was significant enough to justify releasing the aid.[394] He testified:

> I believe Senator Portman was relating, and I believe the Vice President as well, related their view of the importance of the assistance. The Vice President was obviously armed with his conversation with President Zelensky, and they were – they convinced the President that the aid should be disbursed immediately.[395]

Following this meeting, the President decided to lift the pause on U.S. security assistance to Ukraine.[396] The release was conveyed to the interagency the following morning.[397] The U.S. disbursed this assistance without Ukraine ever acting to investigate President Trump's political rival.

Democrats cannot show conclusively that the Trump Administration lifted the pause on security assistance only as a result of their impeachment inquiry. In a private conversation with Senator Johnson on August 31, President Trump signaled that the aid would be released, saying then: "We're reviewing it now, and you'll probably like my final decision."[398] A number of other

---

[390] Deposition of Laura Cooper, in Wash., D.C., at 19, 99 (Oct. 23, 2019).
[391] *Impeachment Inquiry: Ms. Laura Cooper and Mr. David Hale*, *supra* note 246.
[392] Sondland deposition, *supra* note 51, at 106.
[393] Morrison deposition, *supra* note 12, at 242-43.
[394] *Id.* at 243.
[395] *Id.*.
[396] *Id.* at 211.
[397] *Id.*
[398] Letter from Sen. Johnson, *supra* note 138, at 5.

events occurred within the same period. President Zelensky implemented serious anti-corruption reforms in Ukraine and OMB conducted a review of foreign assistance globally and provided data on what other countries contribute to Ukraine. Bipartisan senators contacted the White House, telling the Administration that the Senate would act legislatively to undo the pause on security assistance.[399] In fact, Senator Dick Durbin credited the release of the security assistance to the Senate's potential action.[400] Senator Durbin said, "It's beyond a coincidence that they released it the night before our vote in the committee."[401]

* * *

The evidence does not support the Democrats' allegation that President Trump sought to withhold U.S. security assistance to Ukraine to pressure President Zelensky to investigate his political rival for the President's political benefit. The Democrats' witnesses denied the two were linked. The U.S. officials never informed the Ukrainian government that the security assistance was delayed, and senior Ukrainian officials did not raise concerns to U.S. officials until after the delay was publicly reported. President Trump never raised the security assistance during his phone call with President Zelensky. President Zelensky never voiced concerns about pressure or conditionality on security assistance in any meetings he had with senior U.S. government officials. U.S. security assistance ultimately flowed to Ukraine without the Ukrainian government taking any action to investigate President Trump's political rival.

D. The evidence does not establish that President Trump set up a shadow foreign policy apparatus to pressure Ukraine to investigate the President's political rival for the purpose of benefiting him in the 2020 election.

Democrats allege that President Trump established an unauthorized, so-called "shadow" foreign policy apparatus to pressure Ukraine to investigate his political rival to benefit the President in the 2020 election.[402] Democrats also alleged that President Trump's recall of Ambassador Yovanovitch was a "politically motivated" decision to appease "allies of President Trump."[403] Although the Constitution gives the President broad authority to conduct the foreign policy of the United States, the Democrats say that President Trump abused his power by disregarding the traditional State Department bureaucratic channels for his personal political benefit. These allegations fall flat.

It is impossible to fairly assess the facts without appreciating the circumstances in which they occurred. From the very first days of the Trump Administration—indeed even before it began—the unelected bureaucracy rejected President Trump and his policies. The self-proclaimed "resistance" organized protests and parody social media accounts, while high-level

---

[399] *See* Byron York, *Why did Trump release Ukraine aid? The answer is simple*, Wash. Exam., Nov. 24, 2019.
[400] Caitlin Emma et al., *Trump administration backs off hold on Ukraine military aid*, Politico, Sept. 12, 2019.
[401] *Id.*
[402] Press Release, H. Comm. On Foreign Affairs, Engel Floor Remarks on Resolution for Open Hearings on Trump's Abuse of Power (Oct. 31, 2019); Adam Schiff (@RepAdamSchiff) (Nov. 6, 2019, 10:58 AM), https://twitter.com/RepAdamSchiff/status/1192154367199260672.
[403] Press Release, H. Comm. on Foreign Affairs, Engel & Hoyer Statement on U.S. Ambassador to Ukraine Masha Yovanovitch (May 7, 2019).

bureaucrats received praise from colleagues for openly defying the Administration's policies. Leaks of secret information became almost daily occurrence, including details about the President's sensitive conversations with foreign leaders. Meanwhile, the Department of Justice and FBI spent 22 months thoroughly investigating false allegations that the Trump campaign had colluded with the Russian government in the 2016 election.

The evidence shows that following President Zelensky's inauguration, the three senior U.S. officials who attended his inauguration—Ambassador Kurt Volker, Ambassador Gordon Sondland, and Secretary Rick Perry—assumed responsibility for shepherding the U.S.-Ukrainian relationship. Contrary to assertions of an "irregular" foreign policy channel, all three men were senior U.S. leaders who had important official interests in Ukraine. The three men maintained regular communication with the NSC and the State Department about their work in Ukraine.

Following President Zelensky's inauguration, Ambassador Volker, Ambassador Sondland, and Secretary Perry sought to convince President Trump of Ukraine's commitment to reform. In that meeting, President Trump referenced Mayor Rudy Giuliani, who had experience in Ukraine. When President Zelensky's adviser Andrey Yermak asked Ambassador Volker to connect him with Mayor Giuliani, Ambassador Volker did so because he believed it would advance U.S.-Ukrainian interests. Mayor Giuliani informed Ambassador Volker about his communications with Yermak. Volker and Yermak both have said that Mayor Giuliani did not speak on behalf of the President in these discussions.

Some pockets of the State Department and NSC grumbled that Ambassador Volker, Ambassador Sondland, and Secretary Perry had become so active in U.S-Ukraine policy. Others criticized Ambassador Marie Yovanovitch's recall or fretted about Mayor Giuliani's involvement. Yet, despite these bureaucratic misgivings, there is no evidence that the involvement of Ambassador Volker, Ambassador Sondland, Secretary Perry, or Mayor Giuliani was illegal or hurt U.S. strategic interests. There is also no evidence that President Trump made this arrangement or recalled Ambassador Yovanovitch for the purpose of pressuring Ukraine to investigate the President's political rival for his benefit in the 2020 presidential election.

1. The President has broad Constitutional authority to conduct the foreign policy of the United States.

The Constitution vests the President of the United States with considerable authority over foreign policy.[404] The President is the Commander-in-Chief of U.S. Armed Forces. The President has the power to make treaties with foreign nations, and he appoints and receives "Ambassadors and other public ministers."[405] The Supreme Court has explained that the Constitution gives the President "plenary and exclusive authority" over the conduct of foreign affairs.[406] The President is the "sole organ of the federal government" with respect to foreign affairs.[407]

---

[404] U.S. Const. Art. II.

[405] *Id.*

[406] United States v. Curtiss-Wright Export Corp., 299 U.S. 304, 320 (1936).

[407] *Id.* Although the President makes treaties with the advice and consent of the Senate; the President alone negotiates. *Cf.* H. Jefferson Powell, *The President's Authority Over Foreign Affairs: An Executive Branch Perspective*, 67 Geo. Wash. L. Rev. 527, 546-47 (1999). Dealings with foreign nations require "caution and unity of design," which depend on the President's authority to speak with "one voice" on behalf of U.S. interests. *Id.* at 546.

2. President Trump was likely skeptical of the established national security apparatus as a result of continual leaks and resistance from the federal bureaucracy.

In the wake of President Trump's electoral victory in 2016, he faced almost immediate intransigence from unelected—and often anonymous—federal employees. Since then, the "Resistance" has protested President Trump and leaked sensitive national security information about the Trump Administration's policies and objectives. In this context, one can see how President Trump would be justifiably skeptical of the national security apparatus.

Since the beginning of the Trump Administration, leaks of sensitive national security information have occurred at unprecedented rate. As the *Washington Post* noted, "[e]very presidential administration leaks. So far, the Trump White House has gushed."[408] According to an analysis from the Senate Homeland Security and Governmental Affairs Committee in May 2017, the Trump Administration faced about one national security leak per day—flowing seven times faster in the Trump Administration than during the Obama or Bush Administrations.[409] Unelected bureaucrats leaked details about President Trump's private conversations with world leaders and the investigation into Russian interference in the 2016 election.[410]

In Kimberley Strassel's book *Resistance (At All Costs)*, she described the Resistance as "the legions of Americans who were resolutely opposed to the election of Trump, and who remain angrily determined to remove him from office."[411] This resistance included anonymous federal employees who criticized President Trump and his policies on parody U.S. government social media accounts.[412] This resistance included high-level bureaucrats—including then-Acting Attorney General Sally Yates—who openly defied implementing Administration policies.[413] The resistance included an anonymous employee who published an op-ed in the *New York Times* in September 2018 titled, "I Am Part of the Resistance Inside the Trump Administration," detailing how he or she and other unelected bureaucrats were actively working at odds with the President.[414] The op-ed earned the anonymous employee a book deal.[415]

The "Resistance" extended to the U.S. national security apparatus as well, including FBI agents investigating unproven allegations of collusion between the Trump campaign and the Russian government.[416] An FBI lawyer working the investigation, and later assigned to Special Counsel Robert Mueller's office, texted another FBI employee, "Vive le resistance," in the

---

[408] Paul Farhi, *The Trump administration has sprung a leak. Many of them, in fact*, Wash. Post, Feb. 5, 2017.

[409] Maj. Staff on S. Comm. on Homeland Sec. & Gov't Affairs, 115th Cong., State Secrets: How An Avalanche Of Media Leaks Is Harming National Security (2017) [hereinafter "HSGAC report"].

[410] *Id.*

[411] Kimberley Strassel, Resistance (At All Costs): How Trump Haters Are Breaking America (2019).

[412] Kimberley A. Strassel, *Whistleblowers and the Real Deep State*, Wall St. J., Oct. 11, 2019.

[413] *Id.*

[414] *I Am Part of the Resistance Inside the Trump Administration*, N.Y. Times, Sep. 5, 2018.

[415] Alexa Diaz, *Anonymous Trump official who wrote 'resistance' op-ed to publish tell-all book*, L.A. Times, Oct. 22, 2019.

[416] Special Counsel Robert S. Mueller, III, *Report On The Investigation Into Russian Interference In The 2016 Presidential Election*, 1-2. Vol. 1 (2019) [hereinafter "Mueller report"].

month that President Trump was elected.[417] In the week after election night, FBI Agent Peter Strzok and FBI lawyer Lisa Page—who were both involved in the Russia collusion investigation—wrote to each other: "OMG THIS IS F*CKING TERRIFYING" and "I bought all the president's men. Figure I needed to brush up on watergate [*sic*]."[418]

The FBI surveilled Trump campaign associates using evidence delivered by Christopher Steele—a confidential human source funded by then-candidate Trump's political opponents and who admitted he was "desperate" that Donald Trump lose the election.[419] During her deposition, Dr. Hill testified that Steele's reporting was likely a bogus Russia misinformation campaign against Steele.[420] Yet, the FBI accepted Steele's information and used it to obtain surveillance warrants on Trump campaign associate Carter Page.[421] Ultimately, Special Counsel Mueller's report concluded that the Trump campaign did not conspire or coordinate with Russian election interference actions.[422] In considering the President's mindset, this context cannot be ignored.

3. The President has the constitutional authority to remove Ambassador Yovanovitch.

U.S. ambassadors are the President's representatives abroad, serving at the pleasure of the President. Every ambassador interviewed during this impeachment inquiry recognized and appreciated this fact.[423] Even Ambassador Yovanovitch understood that the President could remove any ambassador at any time for any reason, although she unsurprisingly disagreed with the reason for her removal.[424] The removal of Ambassador Yovanovitch, therefore, is not *per se* evidence of wrongdoing for the President's political benefit.

Evidence suggests that President Trump likely had concerns about Ambassador Yovanovitch's ability to represent him in Ukraine,[425] and that then-Ukrainian President

---

[417] Inspector Gen., Dep't of Justice, *A Review of Various Actions by the Federal Bureau of Investigation and Department of Justice in Advance of the 2016 Election*, 396, 419 (2018).

[418] *Id.* at 397, 400.

[419] F.B.I., Dep't of Just., 302 Interview with Bruce Ohr on Dec. 19, 2016 at 3.

[420] *See* Hill deposition, *supra* note 12, at 177-180 ("I think it was a rabbit hole . . . . The way that the Russians operate is that they will use whatever conduit they can to put out information that is both real and credible but that also masks a great deal of disinformation . . . .").

[421] Transcribed Interview of Sally Moyer, in Wash., D.C., at 162 (Oct. 23, 2018).

[422] Mueller report, *supra* note 416.

[423] Sondland deposition, *supra* note 51, at 19; Volker transcribed interview, *supra* note 60, at 88-89; Transcribed interview of Ambassador Michael McKinley, in Wash., D.C., at 37 (Oct. 16, 2019) [hereinafter "McKinley transcribed interview"]; Yovanovitch deposition, *supra* note 115, at 23; Taylor deposition, *supra* note 47, at 297; Hale deposition, *supra* note 230, at 38.

[424] Yovanovitch deposition, *supra* note 115, at 23. Evidence suggests that Ambassador Yovanovitch took steps to gain the President's trust. Deputy Assistant Secretary of State George Kent testified that Ambassador Yovanovitch taped videos in which she proclaimed support for the Trump Administration's foreign policies. Kent deposition, *supra* note 65, at 118-19. Ambassador Yovanovitch testified that she sought Ambassador Sondland's guidance on how to address negative news reports critical of her work as Ambassador to Ukraine. She said that Ambassador Sondland told her to "go big or go home" in publicly supporting the President. Yovanovitch deposition, *supra* note 115, at 267-28, 306-07. Ambassador Sondland, however, testified that he did not recall advising Ambassador Yovanovitch to make a public statement. Sondland deposition, *supra* note 51, at 58-59.

[425] Memorandum of Telephone Conversation, *supra* note 15.

Poroshenko had authorized an effort to criticize Ambassador Yovanovitch.[426] Ambassador Volker testified that he had no firsthand knowledge of Ambassador Yovanovitch criticizing the President; however, he said that "President Trump would understandably be concerned if that was true because you want to have trust and confidence in your Ambassadors."[427]

Despite recognizing the President's prerogative to dismiss ambassadors, some in the U.S. foreign policy apparatus voiced concerns about Ambassador Yovanovitch's removal. Ambassador McKinley testified that he resigned from the State Department because he believed that it failed to protect its diplomats.[428] However, Ambassador McKinley did not resign when he first learned that Ambassador Yovanovitch had been called home, despite knowing that she had been recalled.[429] He only resigned months later, after the whistleblower's account and the President's comments to President Zelensky about Ambassador Yovanovitch during the July 25 call transcript became public.[430]

Ambassador Yovanovitch testified that her removal from Kyiv had little effect on her career with the State Department. Her post was scheduled to end only a matter of weeks after her recall.[431] Although she had considered extending her tour, a decision had not been officially made.[432] Ambassador Yovanovitch explained that she had been planning to retire following her tour in Ukraine and "[s]o I don't think from a State Department point of view [the recall] has had any effect."[433] The recall also did not affect her compensation.[434] Ambassador Yovanovitch explained that the State Department was helpful in securing her a position with Georgetown University.[435]

4. Ambassador Volker, Ambassador Sondland, and Secretary Perry were all senior U.S. government officers with official interests in Ukraine policy.

Contrary to allegations that President Trump orchestrated a "shadow" foreign policy channel to pressure Ukraine to investigate his political rival, evidence shows that the U.S. interactions with Ukraine were led by senior U.S. officials. These officials, Ambassador Volker, Ambassador Sondland, and Secretary Perry, had attended President Zelensky's inauguration in May 2019 and all had official interests in U.S. policy toward Ukraine.

Ambassador Volker explained that "we viewed ourselves as having been empowered as a Presidential delegation to go there, meet, make an assessment [of whether President Zelensky was a legitimate anti-corruption reformer], and report" to President Trump.[436] He said that they

---

[426] Kent deposition, *supra* note 65, at 232.
[427] Volker transcribed interview, *supra* note 60, at 90.
[428] McKinley transcribed interview, *supra* note 423, at 20, 24-25.
[429] *Id.* at 33-34.
[430] *Id.* at 35-36. *See also* Karen DeYoung, *Senior adviser to Pompeo resigns*, Wash. Post, Oct. 10, 2019.
[431] Yovanovitch deposition, *supra* note 115, at 114-16, 140.
[432] *Id.* at 22, 114-16, 122.
[433] *Id.* at 139-40.
[434] *Impeachment Inquiry: Ambassador Marie Yovanovitch*, *supra* note 4.
[435] Yovanovitch deposition, *supra* note 115, at 139.
[436] Volker transcribed interview, *supra* note 60, at 206.

assumed responsibility to "shepherd this [U.S.-Ukrainian] relationship together as best we could."[437] The delegation assumed this responsibility at a time when the U.S. government lacked an experienced chief of mission in Kyiv.

Importantly, cutting against the idea of a "shadow" channel, each of these three men had an official role with respect to U.S. policy toward Ukraine.[438] Ambassador Volker described his role as the Special Representative for Ukraine Negotiations as "supporting democracy and reform in Ukraine, helping Ukraine better defend itself and deter Russian aggression, and leading U.S. negotiating efforts to end the war and restore Ukraine's territorial integrity."[439] As Ambassador to the European Union, Ambassador Sondland said that Ukraine issues were "central" to his responsibilities.[440] In addition, the Department of Energy, led by Secretary Perry, has significant equities in energy policies in Ukraine.[441]

In the absence of a seasoned chief of mission in Kyiv—before Ambassador Taylor's arrival—these three individuals assumed responsibility following President Zelensky's inauguration for shepherding U.S. engagement with President Zelensky's government. That each individual had an official interest in U.S. policy toward Ukraine undercuts the notion that they engaged in "shadow" diplomacy for illegitimate purposes.

5. Referencing Ukrainian corruption, President Trump told Ambassador Volker, Ambassador Sondland, and Secretary Perry to talk to Mayor Giuliani.

Evidence suggests that Mayor Giuliani's negative assessment of President Zelensky may have reinforced President Trump's existing skepticism about Ukraine and its history of corruption. In May 2019, Mayor Giuliani said that President-elect Zelensky was "surrounded by enemies" of President Trump.[442] When the U.S. delegation to President Zelensky's inauguration later tried to assure President Trump that President Zelensky was different, the President referenced Mayor Giuliani as someone knowledgeable about Ukrainian corruption and told the men to talk to Mayor Giuliani.[443] Testimony differs, however, on whether the President's reference to Mayor Giuliani was a direction or an aside. Either way, because President Trump— constitutionally, the nation's "sole organ of foreign affairs"[444]—raised Mayor Giuliani as

---

[437] *Id.* at 67.

[438] *See Impeachment Inquiry: Dr. Fiona Hill and Mr. David Holmes, supra* note 210.

[439] Volker transcribed interview, *supra* note 60, at 13.

[440] Sondland deposition, *supra* note 51, at 20. During her deposition, Dr. Hill testified that Ambassador Sondland told her that President Trump had "given him broad authority on all things related to Europe, that he was the President's point man on Europe." Hill deposition, *supra* note 12, at 60. Dr. Hill later acknowledged it that Ambassador Sondland could have been exaggerating, explaining that she often saw Ambassador Sondland coming out of West Wing saying he was seeing the President but she learned later that he was really seeing other staff. *Id.* at 204.

[441] James Osborne, *What Rick Perry was doing in Ukraine*, Houston Chronicle, Oct. 16, 2019.

[442] *See* Charles Creitz, *Giuliani cancels Ukraine trip, says he'd be 'walking into a group of people that are enemies of the US,'* Fox News, May 11, 2019.

[443] Sondland deposition, *supra* note 51, at 25. According to public reports, Mayor Giuliani has over a decade of experience working in Ukraine. *See, e.g.*, Rosalind S. Helderman et al., *Impeachment Inquiry Puts New Focus on Giuliani's Work for Prominent Figures in Ukraine,* Wash. Post, Oct. 2, 2019.

[444] *Curtiss-Wright Export Corp.*, 299 U.S. at 320.

someone knowledgeable about Ukraine, this arrangement is not evidence of an unsanctioned and nefarious "shadow" foreign policy apparatus.

On May 23, the U.S. delegation to President Zelensky's inauguration briefed President Trump about their impressions of President Zelensky. Ambassador Sondland testified that the President relayed concerns about Ukrainian corruption, saying "Ukraine is a problem," "tried to take me down," and "talk to Rudy."[445] During his transcribed interview, Ambassador Volker elaborated:

> Q. And can you describe the discussion –
>
> A. Yes.
>
> Q. – that occurred?
>
> A Yes. The President started the meeting and started with kind of a negative assessment of the Ukraine. As I've said earlier –
>
> Q. Yep.
>
> A. – it's a terrible place, all corrupt, terrible people, just dumping on Ukraine.
>
> Q. And they were out to get me in 2016.
>
> A. And they were out to get – and they tried to take me down.
>
> Q. In 2016?
>
> A. Yes. And each of us took turns from this delegation giving our point of view, which was that this is a new crowd, it's a new President, he is committed to doing the right things. I believe I said, he agrees with you. That's why he got elected. It is a terrible place, and he campaigned on cleaning it up, and that's why the Ukrainian people supported him.
>
> So, you know, we strongly encouraged him to engage with this new President because he's committed to fighting all of those things that President Trump was complaining about.
>
> Q. And how did the President react?
>
> A. He just didn't believe it. He was skeptical. And he also said, that's not what I hear. I hear, you know, he's got some terrible people

---

[445] Sondland deposition, *supra* note 51, at 61-62, 75.

71

around him. And he referenced that he hears from Mr. Giuliani as part of that.

Q. Can you explain a little bit more about what the President said about Rudy Giuliani in that meeting?

A. He said that's not what I hear. I hear a whole bunch of other things. And I don't know how he phrased it with Rudy, but it was – I think he said, not as an instruction but just as a comment, talk to Rudy, you know. He knows all of these things, and they've got some bad people around him. And that was the nature of it. It was clear that he also had other sources. It wasn't only Rudy Giuliani. I don't know who those might be, but he – or at least he said, I hear from people.[446]

In his public testimony, Ambassador Volker reiterated that he did not understand the President's comment, "talk to Rudy," to be a direction.[447] He explained:

I didn't take it as an instruction. I want to be clear about that. He said: That's not what I hear. You know, when we were giving him our assessment about President Zelensky and where Ukraine is headed: That's not what I hear. I hear terrible things. He's got terrible people around him. Talk to Rudy. And I understood, in that context, him just saying that's where he hears it from. I didn't take it as an instruction."[448]

Ambassador Sondland, however, in both his closed-door deposition and his public testimony, characterized the President's comment as a "direction."[449] In an interview with the *Wall Street Journal*, Energy Secretary Rick Perry stated that he called Mayor Giuliani following the May 23 meeting, and that Mayor Giuliani told him "to be careful with regards" to President Zelensky.[450] Secretary Perry said "he never heard the president, any of his appointees, Mr. Giuliani, or the Ukrainian regime discuss the possibility of specifically investigating former Vice President Joe Biden, a Democratic presidential contender, and his son Hunter Biden."[451]

---

[446] Volker transcribed interview, *supra* note 60, at 304-05. Deputy Assistant Secretary Kent testified that Dr. Hill relayed to him that President Trump had conversations with Viktor Orban, the Prime Minister of Hungary, and Vladimir Putin, the President of Russia, which he said may have also colored President Trump's view of Ukraine. Kent deposition, *supra* note 65, at 253-54.

[447] *Impeachment Inquiry: Ambassador Kurt Volker and Mr. Timothy Morrison, supra* note 8.

[448] *Id.*

[449] *Impeachment Inquiry: Ambassador Gordon Sondland, supra* note 56; Sondland deposition, *supra* note 51, at 25-26.

[450] Timothy Puko & Rebecca Ballhaus, *Rick Perry called Rudy Giuliani at Trump's direction on Ukraine concerns*, Wall St. J., Oct. 16, 2019.

[451] *Id.*

6. At the Ukrainian government's request, Ambassador Volker connected them with Mayor Giuliani to change his impression about the Zelensky regime.

Evidence shows that the Ukrainian government, and specifically Zelensky adviser Andrey Yermak, initiated contact with Mayor Giuliani—and not the other way around—to attempt to refute Mayor Giuliani's views about President Zelensky. Yermak later told *Bloomberg* that he had informed both Republicans and Democrats in Congress in July 2019 that he planned to engage with Mayor Giuliani and heard no objections.[452]

According to Ambassador Volker, in May 2019, he "became concerned that a negative narrative about Ukraine fueled by assertions made by Ukraine's departing prosecutor general" was reaching President Trump via Mayor Giuliani.[453] In July, Ambassador Volker shared his concerns with Yermak, who asked Ambassador Volker to connect him with Mayor Giuliani directly.[454] Ambassador Volker explained:

> After sharing my concerns with the Ukrainian leadership, an adviser to President Zelensky asked me to connect him to the President's personal lawyer, Mayor Rudy Giuliani. I did so. I did so solely because I understood that the new Ukrainian leadership wanted to convince those, like Mayor Giuliani, who believed such a negative narrative about Ukraine, that times have changed and that, under President Zelensky, Ukraine is worthy of U.S. support. I also made clear to the Ukrainians on a number of occasions that Mayor Giuliani is a private citizen and the President's personal lawyer and that he does not represent the United States Government.[455]

Ambassador Volker was clear during his transcribed interview that his action connecting Yermak with Mayor Giuliani was in the best interests of the United States. He testified:

> Q. And so any of the facts here, you connecting Mr. Giuliani with Mr. Yermak and to the extent you were facilitating Mr. Giuliani's communication with anybody in the Ukraine, you were operating under the best interests of the United States?
>
> A. Absolutely.
>
> Q. And to the extent Mr. Giuliani is tight with the President, has a good relationship with him, has the ability to influence him, is it fair to say that, at times, it was in the U.S.'s interest to have Mr. Giuliani connecting with these Ukrainian officials?

---

[452] Baker & Krasnolutska, *supra* note 280.
[453] Volker transcribed interview, *supra* note 60, at 18.
[454] *Id.*; *see also id.* at 137-38.
[455] *Id.* at 18.

A. Yes. I would say it this way: It was I think in the U.S. interest for the information that was reaching the President to be accurate and fresh and coming from the right people. And if some of what Mr. Giuliani believed or heard from, for instance, the former [Ukrainian] Prosecutor General Lutsenko was self-serving, inaccurate, wrong, et cetera, I think correcting that perception that he has is important, because to the extent that the President does hear from him, as he would, you don't want this dissonant information reaching the President.[456]

In an interview with *Bloomberg*, Yermak explained that he sought to engage with Mayor Giuliani to "dispel the notion that the new Ukraine government was corrupt."[457] Yermak said the Zelensky regime was "surprised" that Mayor Giuliani believed them to be "enemies of the U.S." and they sought to ask Mayor Giuliani directly why he believed that.[458] Yermak recounted how, before his engaged with Mayor Giuliani, he sought bipartisan feedback from Congress about this approach.[459] He said that he spoke with "the top national security advisers to the minority and majority leaders in both the U.S. House and Senate" and told them that "he planned to talk to [Mayor] Giuliani to explain the nation's reform agenda and to urge him not to communicate with Ukraine through the media."[460] Yermak recalled, "Everyone said: 'good idea.'"[461]

7. The Ukrainian government understood that Mayor Giuliani was not speaking on behalf of President Trump.

Ambassador Volker was the chief interlocutor with the Ukrainian government. He described himself as someone who had the Ukrainian government's trust and who offered them counsel on how to address the negative narrative about Ukrainian corruption.[462] Ambassador Volker testified that the Ukrainian government did not view Mayor Giuliani as President Trump's "agent" on whose behalf he spoke.[463] Instead, the Ukrainians saw Mayor Giuliani as a one-way method for conveying information to President Trump about President Zelensky's commitment to reform.

Under examination by House Intelligence Committee Chairman Adam Schiff in his closed-door deposition, Ambassador Volker was resolute that the Ukrainian government saw Mayor Giuliani as someone who "had the President's ear," not someone who spoke for the President. He explained:

Q. You understood that the Ukrainians recognized that Rudy Giuliani represented the President, that he was an agent of the President, that

---

[456] *Id.* at 69-70.
[457] Baker & Krasnolutska, *supra* note 280.
[458] *Id.*
[459] *Id.*
[460] *Id.*
[461] *Id.*
[462] Volker transcribed interview, *supra* note 60, at 168-69.
[463] *Id.* at 116.

he was a direct channel to the President. Ukrainian officials you were dealing with would have understood that, would they not?

A. *I would not say that they thought of him as an agent*, but that he was a way of communicating, that you could get something to Giuliani and he would be someone who would be talking to the President anyway, so it would flow information that way.

Q. So this was someone who had the President's ear?

A. Yes. That's fair.[464]

In his public testimony, Ambassador Volker reiterated that Mayor Giuliani was not speaking on the President's behalf. He explained:

> I made clear to the Ukrainians that Mayor Giuliani was a private citizen, the President's personal lawyer, and not representing the U.S. Government. Likewise, in my conversations with Mayor Giuliani, I never considered him to be speaking on the President's behalf, or giving instructions. Rather, the information flow was the other way, from Ukraine to Mayor Giuliani, in the hopes that this would clear up the information reaching President Trump.[465]

During her closed-door deposition, Dr. Hill confirmed this assessment, explaining that she could not say that Mayor Giuliani was acting on President Trump's behalf.[466]

Andrey Yermak, in an August 2019 *New York Times* article, said it was also not clear to him whether Mayor Giuliani was speaking on behalf of President Trump.[467] According to the *Times*, Mayor Giuliani "explicitly stated that he was not" speaking on behalf of the President.[468] President Trump confirmed this fact in a November 2019 interview, explaining that he did not direct Mayor Giuliani's Ukraine activities.[469]

8. Ambassador Volker, Ambassador Sondland, and Secretary Perry kept the National Security Council and the State Department informed about their actions.

As Ambassador Volker, Ambassador Sondland, and Secretary Perry engaged with Ukrainian government officials, they maintained communications with the State Department and NSC. This coordination undercuts any notion that President Trump orchestrated a "shadow" foreign policy apparatus to work outside of the State Department or NSC.

---

[464] *Id.* (emphasis added).

[465] *Impeachment Inquiry: Ambassador Kurt Volker and Mr. Timothy Morrison, supra* note 8.

[466] Hill deposition, *supra* note 12, at 424-25.

[467] Kramer & Vogel, *supra* note 176.

[468] *Id.*

[469] Daniel Chaitin, *'I didn't direct him': Trump denies sending Giuliani to Ukraine,* Wash. Exam., Nov. 26, 2019.

Ambassador Volker testified that "while executing my duties, I kept my colleagues at the State Department and National Security Council informed and also briefed Congress about my actions."[470] Ambassador Volker and Ambassador Sondland also communicated regularly with Ambassador Bill Taylor once he became the chargé d'affaires, *a.i.*, in Kyiv.[471] These briefings went as high as the Counselor to the Secretary of State, Ulrich Brechbuhl.[472]

In his public testimony, Ambassador Sondland explained that it was "no secret" what he, Ambassador Volker, and Secretary Perry were doing. As he stated, "[w]e kept the NSC apprised of our efforts, including specifically our efforts to secure a public statement from the Ukrainians that would satisfy President Trump's concerns."[473] Ambassador Sondland testified that "everyone was in the loop," although he conceded that he "presumed" a connection between investigations and security assistance without speaking to President Trump, Acting Chief of Staff Mulvaney, or Mayor Giuliani.[474]

9. Although some in the U.S. foreign policy establishment bristled, the roles of Ambassador Volker, Ambassador Sondland, and Secretary Perry and their interactions with Mayor Giuliani did not violate the law or harm national security.

Evidence suggests that some in the U.S. foreign policy establishment disliked the involvement of Ambassador Volker, Ambassador Sondland, and Secretary Perry in the U.S.-Ukrainian relationship. Some also expressed discomfort with Mayor Giuliani's interactions with Ukrainian officials. However, the use of private citizens, such as Mayor Giuliani, to assist effectuating U.S. foreign policy goals on specific issues is not *per se* inappropriate and the Democrats' witnesses testified that the use of private citizens can sometimes beneficial. There is no evidence that the arrangement here violated any laws or harmed national security.

Some of the Democrats' witnesses criticized the non-traditional diplomacy. Ambassador Taylor testified about his concern for what he characterized as "two channels" of U.S. policy-making in Ukraine: a regular, State Department channel and an "irregular, informal" channel featuring Ambassador Volker, Ambassador Sondland, Secretary Perry, and Mayor Giuliani.[475] Deputy Assistant Secretary Kent testified that he was concerned that discussions were occurring outside the "formal policy process."[476]

Dr. Hill, too, disapproved of a non-traditional channel of communication, testifying that she disagreed with Ambassador Volker's decision to engage with Mayor Giuliani.[477] Dr. Hill

---

[470] Volker transcribed interview, *supra* note 60, at 19.
[471] *See generally* text messages exchanged between Kurt Volker and Gordon Sondland [KV00000036-39].
[472] Volker transcribed interview, *supra* note 60, at 59.
[473] *Impeachment Inquiry: Ambassador Gordon Sondland, supra* note 56.
[474] *Id.*
[475] Taylor deposition, *supra* note 47, at 23-24.
[476] Kent deposition, *supra* note 65, at 266-67.
[477] Hill deposition, *supra* note 12, at 113-14. Ambassador Sondland recounted that when he met with Dr. Hill prior to her departure from the White House in mid-July, she was "pretty upset about her role" in the Administration and

characterized Ambassador Sondland's conduct as a "domestic political errand."[478] However, by the time that Dr. Hill left the NSC on July 19, Ambassador Volker had only met with Mayor Giuliani once and Ambassador Sondland had never communicated with him.[479] Mayor Giuliani did not meet with the Ukrainian government until early August.[480]

Despite this criticism, Ambassador Volker said that Ambassador Taylor never raised concerns to him about an "irregular" foreign policy channel.[481] The Democrats' witnesses also explained that unorthodox foreign policy channels are not unusual and can actually be helpful to advance U.S. interests. Ambassador Taylor testified that non-traditional channels of diplomacy "can be helpful."[482] Ambassador Volker testified that he always operated with the best interests of the U.S. in mind and to advance "U.S. foreign policy goals with respect to Ukraine."[483]

The impeachment inquiry has uncovered no clear evidence that President Trump directed Ambassador Volker, Ambassador Sondland, and Secretary Perry to work with Mayor Giuliani for the purpose of pressuring Ukraine to investigate his political rival. In fact, the evidence suggests that the White House actively worked to stop potential impropriety. When Mayor Giuliani attempted to obtain a visa for former Ukrainian Prosecutor General Viktor Shokin to travel to the U.S. in January 2019, the White House shut down the effort.[484] The State Department had denied Shokin's visa and Mayor Giuliani apparently appealed to the White House.[485] According to Deputy Assistant Secretary Kent, in settling the matter, White House senior advisor Rob Blair said: "I heard what I need to know to protect the interest of the President."[486] Shokin did not receive a visa.

*   *   *

The evidence does not support the Democrats' allegation that President Trump set up a shadow foreign policy apparatus to pressure Ukraine to investigate the President's political rival for his political benefit in the 2020 election. The Constitution vests the President with broad authority over U.S. foreign relations. The U.S. officials accused of conducting "shadow" foreign policy—Ambassador Volker, Ambassador Sondland, and Secretary Perry—were all senior leaders with official interests in Ukraine who informed the State Department and NSC of their actions. Mayor Giuliani, whom President Trump referenced in the May 23 meeting with these three U.S. officials, also had experience in Ukraine.

---

so mad that Ambassador Sondland said he had "never seen anyone so upset." Sondland deposition, *supra* note 51, at 266-67, 307. In her public testimony, Dr. Hill explained that she was angry with Ambassador Sondland for not coordinating with her sufficiently. *Impeachment Inquiry: Dr. Fiona Hill and Mr. David Holmes, supra* note 210.

[478] *Impeachment Inquiry: Dr. Fiona Hill and Mr. David Holmes, supra* note 210.

[479] *Impeachment Inquiry: Ambassador Kurt Volker and Mr. Timothy Morrison, supra* note 8; *Impeachment Inquiry: Ambassador Gordon Sondland, supra* note 56.

[480] *Impeachment Inquiry: Ambassador Kurt Volker and Mr. Timothy Morrison, supra* note 8.

[481] *Impeachment Inquiry: Ambassador Kurt Volker and Mr. Timothy Morrison, supra* note 8.

[482] Taylor deposition, *supra* note 47, at 177.

[483] Volker transcribed interview, *supra* note 60, at 15, 69.

[484] Kent deposition, *supra* note 65, at 48-49.

[485] *Id.* at 48-49.

[486] *Id.* at 143.

The Ukrainian government asked Ambassador Volker to connect them with Mayor Giuliani to help change Mayor Giuliani's skeptical view of President Zelensky and "clear up" information flowing to the President. The Ukrainian government saw Mayor Giuliani as someone who had the President's ear but they did not see him as speaking on behalf of the President. While some in the U.S. foreign policy establishment disagreed with these actions, there is no indication it harmed national security or violated any laws. Notably, Ambassador Volker said he operated at all times with the U.S. national interest in mind. Ultimately, Ukraine took no actions to investigate President Trump's political rival.

E. President Trump is not wrong to raise questions about Hunter Biden's role with Burisma or Ukrainian government officials' efforts to influence the 2016 campaign.

Democrats allege that President Trump and Mayor Giuliani are spreading "conspiracy theories" by raising questions about Hunter Biden's role on the board of Burisma and certain Ukrainian government officials' efforts to influence the 2016 election.[487] The evidence available, however, shows that there are legitimate, unanswered questions about both issues. As Ukraine implements anti-corruption reforms, it is appropriate for the country to examine these allegations.

The Democrats' witnesses described how Burisma has long been a subject of controversy in Ukraine. The company's founder, Mykola Zlochevsky, was Ukraine's Minister of Ecology and Natural Resources from 2010 to 2012. In that role, he allegedly granted Burisma licenses for certain mineral deposits. Hunter Biden and other well-connected Democrats joined Burisma's board at a time when the company faced criticism. Hunter Biden's role on Burisma was concerning enough to the Obama State Department that it raised the issue with Vice President Biden's office and even prepared Ambassador Yovanovitch for a potential question on the topic at her confirmation hearing in 2016.

The extent of Ukraine's involvement in the 2016 election draws a much more visceral denial from Democrats, despite harsh rhetoric from prominent Democrats condemning foreign interference in U.S. election. It is undisputed that the then-Ukraine Ambassador to the U.S. authored an op-ed criticizing candidate Trump in U.S. media at the height of the presidential campaign. It is undisputed that senior Ukrainian officials made negative and critical comments about candidate Trump. In addition, a well-researched January 2017 article in *Politico* chronicles attempts by some Ukrainian government officials to harm candidate Trump. The article quotes a former DNC contractor and Ukrainian embassy staffer to show how the Ukrainian embassy worked with Democrat operatives and the media to hurt President Trump's candidacy.

1. It is appropriate for Ukraine to investigate allegations of corruption in its country.

As Ukraine adopts anti-corruption reforms, the United States has encouraged the country's leaders to investigate and prosecute corruption. Deputy Assistant Secretary of State for

---

[487] *See, e.g., Impeachment Inquiry: Ambassador Gordon Sondland, supra* note 56; *Impeachment Inquiry: Ambassador William B. Taylor and Mr. George Kent, supra* note 2;

European and Eurasian Affairs George Kent described Ukraine's corruption problem as "serious" and said corruption has long been "part of the high-level dialogue" between the United States and Ukraine.[488] Ambassador Marie Yovanovitch, the former U.S. Ambassador to Ukraine, testified that in Ukraine "corruption is not just prevalent, but frankly is the system."[489] Although Ukraine has established various anti-corruption prosecutors, courts, and investigative agencies to address the pervasive problem, corruption remains a problem.[490]

The Democrats' witnesses testified that it is appropriate for Ukraine to investigate allegations of corruption, including allegations about Burisma and 2016 election influence. Dr. Fiona Hill, Senior Director for Europe at the NSC, explained that it is "not actually . . . completely ridiculous" for President Zelensky's administration to investigate allegations of corruption arising from prior Ukrainian administrations.[491] Ambassador Volker testified that he "always thought [it] was fine" for Ukraine to investigate allegations about 2016 election influence.[492] Ambassador Yovanovitch testified:

> Q. Ambassador Volker mentioned the fact that to the extent there are corrupt Ukrainians and the United States is advocating for the Ukraine to investigate themselves, that certainly would be an appropriate initiative for U.S. officials to advocate for. Is that right?
>
> A. If that's what took place.[493]

With President Trump's deep-seated and genuine concern about corruption in Ukraine, it is not unreasonable that he would raise two examples of concern in a conversation with President Zelensky. Democrats are fundamentally wrong to argue that President Trump urged President Zelensky to "manufacture" or "dig up" "dirt" by raising these issues. As Ambassador Volker testified:

> Q. Would you say that President Trump in the phone call – and you've read the transcript and you're familiar with all the parties – was asking President Zelensky to manufacture dirt on the Bidens?
>
> A. No. And I've seen that phrase thrown around a lot. And I think there's a difference between the manufacture or dig up dirt versus finding out did anything happen in the 2016 campaign or did anything happen with Burisma. I think – or even if he's asking them to investigate the Bidens, it is to find out what facts there may be rather than to manufacture something.

---

[488] Kent deposition, *supra* note 65, at 105, 151.
[489] Yovanovitch deposition, *supra* note 115, at 18.
[490] *Id.* at 79-80.
[491] Hill deposition, *supra* note 12, at 394.
[492] Volker transcribed interview, *supra* note 60, at 146.
[493] Yovanovitch deposition, *supra* note 115, at 294.

Q. It is not an accurate statement of what the President was asking Ukraine to sum it up as saying that President Trump was asking Ukraine to manufacture dirt?

A. Yeah, I agree with that.[494]

2. There are legitimate concerns surrounding Hunter Biden's position on the board of Ukrainian energy company Burisma during his father's term as Vice President of the United States.

Burisma Holdings had a reputation in Ukraine as a corrupt company.[495] The company was founded by Mykola Zlochevsky, who served as Ukraine's Minister of Ecology and Natural Resources from 2010 to 2012.[496] During Zlochevsky's tenure in the Ukrainian government, Burisma received oil exploration licenses without public auctions.[497]

According to the *New York Times*, Hunter Biden and two other well-connected Democrats—Christopher Heinz, then-Secretary of State John Kerry's stepson, and Devon Archer—"were part of a broad effort by Burisma to bring in well-connected Democrats during a period when the company was facing investigations backed not just by domestic Ukrainian forces but by officials in the Obama administration."[498] Hunter Biden joined Burisma's board when his father, Vice President Joe Biden, acted as the Obama Administration's point person on Ukraine.[499]

The appearance of a conflict of interest raised concerns during the Obama Administration. In May 2014, the *Washington Post* reported "[t]he appointment of the vice president's son to a Ukrainian oil board looks nepotistic at best, nefarious at worst. No matter how qualified Biden is, it ties into the idea that U.S. foreign policy is self-interested, and that's a narrative Vladimir Putin has pushed during Ukraine's crisis."[500] The *Post* likened Hunter Biden's position with Burisma to "children of Russian politicians" who take "executive positions in companies at the top of the Forbes 500 list, and China's 'princelings' [who] have a similar habit."[501]

Deputy Assistant Secretary of State George Kent testified that while he served as acting Deputy Chief of Mission in Kyiv in early 2015, he raised concerns directly to Vice President Biden's office about Hunter Biden's service on Burisma's board.[502] Kent said that the "message"

---

[494] Volker transcribed interview, *supra* note 60, at 212-213.

[495] Kent deposition, *supra* note 65, at 83.

[496] Paul Sonne & Laura Mills, *Ukrainians see conflict in Biden's anticorruption message*, Wall St. J., Dec. 7, 2015.

[497] *Id.*

[498] Kenneth P. Vogel & Iuliia Mendel, *Biden faces conflicts of interest questions that are being promoted by Trump and allies*, N.Y. Times, May 1, 2019.

[499] Adam Taylor, *Hunter Biden's new job at a Ukrainian gas company is a problem for U.S. soft power*, Wash. Post, May 14, 2014.

[500] *Id.*

[501] *Id.*

[502] Kent deposition, *supra* note 65, at 226-27.

he received back was that because Vice President Biden's elder son, Beau, was dying of brain cancer at the time, there was no "bandwidth" to deal with any other family issues.[503]

In December 2015, the *Wall Street Journal* reported that Ukrainian anti-corruption activists complained that Vice President Biden's anti-corruption message "is being undermined as his son receives money" from Zlochevsky.[504] According to the *Journal*, "some anticorruption campaigners here [in Kyiv] worry the link with Mr. Biden may protect Mr. Zlochevsky from being prosecuted in Ukraine."[505]

Ambassador Yovanovitch testified that the Obama State Department actually prepared her to address Hunter Biden's role on Burisma if she received a question about it during her Senate confirmation hearing to be ambassador to Ukraine in June 2016. She explained:

> Q. And you may have mentioned this when we were speaking before lunch, but when did the issues related to Burisma first get to your attention? Was that as soon as you arrived in country?
>
> A. Not really. I first became aware of it when I was being prepared for my Senate confirmation hearing. So I'm sure you're familiar with the concept of questions and answer and various other things. And so there was one there about Burisma, and so, you know, that's when I first heard that word.
>
> Q. Were there any other companies that were mentioned in connection with Burisma?
>
> A. I don't recall.
>
> Q. And was it in the general sense of corruption, there was a company bereft with corruption?
>
> A. The way the question was phrased in this model Q&A was, what can you tell us about Hunter Biden's, you know, being named to the board of Burisma?
>
>   ***
>
> Q. Did anyone at the State Department – when you were coming on board as the new ambassador, did anyone at the State Department brief you about this tricky issue, that Hunter Biden was on the board of this company and the company suffered from allegations of corruption, and provide you guidance?

---

[503] *Id.*
[504] Sonne & Mills, *supra*, note 496.
[505] *Id.*

A. Well, there was that Q&A that I mentioned.[506]

According to testimony, the Obama State Department actually took steps to prevent the U.S. government from associating with Burisma. In his closed-door deposition, Deputy Assistant Secretary Kent recounted a story about how he stopped a taxpayer-funded partnership with Burisma in mid-2016.[507] He said he learned that Burisma sought to cosponsor a U.S. Agency for International Development (USAID) program to encourage Ukrainian school children to develop ideas for clean energy.[508] Kent said he advised USAID not to work with Burisma due to its reputation for corruption.[509]

U.S. law enforcement in the past has examined employment arrangements in which a company hires a seemingly unqualified individual to influence government action. In 2016, the Obama Justice Department fined a Hong Kong subsidiary of a multinational bank for a scheme similar to Burisma's use of Hunter Biden and other well-connected Democrats.[510] There, the company hired otherwise unqualified candidates to "influence" officials toward favorable business outcomes.[511] At the time, then-Assistant Attorney General Leslie Caldwell explained that "[a]warding prestigious employment opportunities to unqualified individuals in order to influence government officials is corruption, plain and simple."[512]

During their public testimony, Democrat witnesses testified that Hunter Biden's role on Burisma's board of directors created the potential for the appearance of a conflict of interest. LTC Vindman testified that Hunter Biden did not appear qualified to serve on Burisma's board.[513] Deputy Assistant Secretary Kent explained that the issues surrounding Burisma were worthy of investigation by Ukrainian authorities.[514] Kent testified:

Q. But given Hunter Biden's role on Burisma's board of directors, at some point, you testified in your deposition that you expressed some concern to the Vice President's office. Is that correct?

A. That is correct.

Q. And what did they do about that concern that you expressed?

A. I have no idea. I reported my concern to the Office of the Vice President.

---

[506] Yovanovitch deposition, *supra* note 115, at 150-53.
[507] Kent deposition, *supra* note 65, at 88, 102-03.
[508] *Id.* at 103
[509] *Id.* at 102.
[510] Press Release, U.S. Dep't of Justice, JPMorgan's Investment Bank in Hong Kong Agrees to Pay $72 Million Penalty for Corrupt Hiring Scheme in China (Nov. 17, 2016), https://www.justice.gov/opa/pr/jpmorgan-s-investment-bank-hong-kong-agrees-pay-72-million-penalty-corrupt-hiring-scheme.
[511] *Id.*
[512] *Id.*
[513] *Impeachment Inquiry: LTC Alexander Vindman and Ms. Jennifer Williams, supra* note 6.
[514] *Impeachment Inquiry: Ambassador William B. Taylor and Mr. George Kent, supra* note 2.

Q. Okay. That was the end of it? Nobody –

A. Sir, you would have to ask people who worked in the Office of the Vice President during 2015.

Q. But after you expressed a concern of a perceived conflict of interest, at the least, the Vice President's engagement in the Ukraine didn't decrease, did it?

A. Correct, because the Vice President was promoting U.S. policy objectives in Ukraine.

Q. And Hunter Biden's role on the board of Burisma didn't cease, did it?

A. To the best of my knowledge, it didn't. And my concern was that there was the possibility of a perception of a conflict of interest.[515]

Similarly, in her public testimony, Ambassador Yovanovitch agreed that concerns about Hunter Biden's presence on Burisma's board were legitimate. In an exchange with Rep. Ratcliffe, she testified:

Q. You understood from Deputy Assistant Secretary George Kent's testimony, as it's been related to you that he testified a few days ago, do you understand that that arrangement, Hunter Biden's role on the Burisma board, caused him enough concern that, as he testified in his statement, that "in February of 2015, I raised my concern that Hunter Biden's status as a board member could create the perception of a conflict of interest." Then he went on to talk about the Vice President's responsibilities over the Ukraine – or over Ukraine – Ukrainian policy as one of those factors. Do you recall that?

A. Yes.

Q. Did you ever – do you agree with that?

A. Yes.

Q. That it was a legitimate concern to raise?

A. I think that it could raise the appearance of a conflict of interest.

***

---

[515] *Id.*

Q. But the legitimate concern about Hunter Biden's role was legitimate, correct?

A. I think it creates a concern that there could be an appearance of conflict of interest.[516]

During her public testimony, Dr. Hill testified:

Q. Dr. Hill, you told us during your deposition that, indeed, that there are perceived conflict of interest troubles when the child of a government official is involved with something that government official has an official policy role in, correct?

A. I think any family member of any member of the U.S. Government, Congress or the Senate, is open to all kinds of questions about optics and of perhaps undue outside influence, if they take part in any kind of activity that could be misconstrued as being related to their parent or the family member's work. So as a matter of course, yes, I do think that's the case.[517]

Despite this evidence, House Intelligence Committee Chairman Adam Schiff has prevented Republican Members from fully assessing the role of Hunter Biden on Burisma's board of directors. Chairman Schiff refused to invite Hunter Biden and Devon Archer to testify during public hearings.[518] Chairman Schiff declined to concur with a Republican subpoena for Hunter Biden to testify in a closed-door deposition.[519] Chairman Schiff declined to concur with a Republican subpoena for documents relating to Hunter Biden's role on Burisma.[520]

In addition to Burisma, there are questions about why the Ukrainian government fired then-Prosecutor General Shokin—according to Vice President Biden, at his insistence[521]—when it did not fire his successor, Prosecutor General Yuriy Lutsenko. Although Shokin and Lutsenko were both seen by State Department officials as corrupt and ineffective prosecutors, there was no effort to remove Lutsenko to the same degree or in the same way as there was with Shokin.[522] Ambassador Yovanovitch testified:

Q. And was he, in your experience – because you're very knowledgeable about the region, so when I ask you in your opinion, you have a very informed opinion – was Lutsenko better or worse than Shokin?

---

[516] *Impeachment Inquiry: Ambassador Marie Yovanovitch, supra* note 4.

[517] *Impeachment Inquiry: Dr. Fiona Hill and Mr. David Holmes, supra* note 210.

[518] *See, e.g.,* Allan Smith, *Democrats push back on GOP effort to have whistleblower, Hunter Biden testify,* NBC News, Nov. 10, 2019.

[519] *Impeachment Inquiry: Ms. Laura Cooper and Mr. David Hale, supra* note 246.

[520] *Id.*

[521] Council on Foreign Relations, Foreign Affairs Issue Launch with Former Vice President Joe Biden (Jan. 23, 2018).

[522] Kent deposition, *supra* note 65, at 90-98, 144-49.

A. I mean, honestly, I don't know. I mean, I think they're cut from the same cloth.

***

Q. There was never as much of a clamor to remove Lutsenko as there was Shokin. Is that fair to say?

A. Yeah, I think that's fair.

Q. And what do you account for that?

A. I would say that there was, I think, still a hope that one could work with Mr. Lutsenko. There was also that prospect of Presidential elections coming up, and as seemed likely by, you know, December, January, February, whatever the time was, that there would be a change of government. And I think we certainly hoped that Mr. Lutsenko would be replaced in the natural order of things, which is, in fact, what happened. We also had more leverage before. I mean, this was not easy. President Poroshenko and Mr. Shokin go way back. In fact, I think that they are godfathers to each other's children. So this was, you know, this was a big deal. But we had assistance, as did the IMF, that we could condition.[523]

Evidence suggests that Lutsenko's misconduct was not trivial. Deputy Assistant Secretary Kent explained that the U.S. government became disillusioned with Lutsenko in 2017 when he exposed an undercover investigator working to catch Ukrainian government officials selling fraudulent biometric passports.[524] Kent said that Lutsenko's actions could have resulted in terrorists obtaining fraudulent biometric passports.[525] Whereas Shokin only served for little over a year, Lutsenko served for years until President Zelensky removed him.[526] Although both prosecutors were regarded as ineffective and corrupt, the U.S. government only took an official position with respect to Shokin's removal and never as to Lutsenko's.[527]

3. There are legitimate questions about the extent to which Ukrainian government officials worked to oppose President Trump's candidacy in the 2016 election.

Democrats reflexively oppose any discussion about whether senior Ukrainian government officials worked to oppose President Trump's candidacy and support former Secretary Clinton during the 2016 election. Calling these allegations "debunked" and "conspiracy theories," Democrats ignore irrefutable evidence that is inconvenient for their

---

[523] Yovanovitch deposition, *supra* note 115, at 102-03.
[524] Kent deposition, *supra* note 65, at 145-47.
[525] *Id.* at 147-48.
[526] *Id.* at 95-103.
[527] *Id.* at 95.

political narrative. The facts, however, show outstanding questions about Ukrainian influence in the 2016 presidential election—questions that the Democrats' witnesses said would be appropriate for Ukraine to examine.

Prominent Democrats expressed concern about foreign interference in U.S. elections when they believed that the Russian government colluded with the Trump campaign in 2016. For example, in a 2017 hearing about Russian election interference, then-Ranking Member Schiff said that the "stakes are nothing less than the future of liberal democracy."[528] But where evidence suggests that Ukraine also sought to influence the election to the benefit of the Clinton campaign, now-Chairman Schiff and fellow Democrats have held their outrage.

Democrats have posited a false choice: that influence in the 2016 election is binary—it could have been conducted by Russia or by Ukraine, but not both. This is nonsense. Under then-Chairman Devin Nunes, Republicans on the House Intelligence Committee issued a report in March 2018 detailing Russia's active measures campaign against the United States.[529] But Russian interference in U.S. elections does not preclude Ukrainian officials from also attempting to influence the election. As Ambassador Volker testified during his public hearing, it is possible for more than one country to influence U.S. elections.[530]

Indisputable evidence shows that senior Ukrainian government officials sought to influence the 2016 election in favor of Secretary Clinton and against then-candidate Trump. In August 2016, then-Ukrainian Ambassador to the United States, Valeriy Chaly, wrote an op-ed in *The Hill* criticizing Trump's policies toward Ukraine.[531] The same month, the *Financial Times* reported that Trump's candidacy led "Kyiv's wider political leadership to do something they would never have attempted before: intervene, however indirectly, in a US election."[532] Ukrainian parliamentarian Serhiy Leshchenko explained that Ukraine was "on Hillary Clinton's side.[533] Other senior Ukrainian officials called candidate Trump a "clown," a "dangerous misfit," and "dangerous," and alleged that candidate Trump "challenged the very values of the free world."[534]

Other publicly available information reinforces the conclusion that senior Ukrainian government officials worked in 2016 to support Secretary Clinton. A January 2017 *Politico* article by current-*New York Times* reporter Ken Vogel detailed the Ukrainian effort to "sabotage" the Trump campaign.[535] Although Democrats reflexively dismiss the information presented in this article, neither *Politico* nor Vogel have retracted the story.

---

[528] *Open hearing on Russian Active Measures Campaign: Hearing before the H. Perm. Sel. Comm. on Intelligence*, 115th Cong. (2017)

[529] H. Perm. Sel. Comm. on Intelligence, Report on Russian Active Measures (Mar. 2018).

[530] *Impeachment Inquiry: Ambassador Kurt Volker and Mr. Timothy Morrison, supra* note 8

[531] *See* Chaly, *supra* note 27.

[532] Olearchyk, *supra* note 123.

[533] *Id.*

[534] *Id.*; Vogel & Stern, *supra* note 127.

[535] Vogel & Stern, *supra* note 127.

According to Vogel's reporting, the Ukrainian government worked with a Democrat operative and the media in 2016 to boost Secretary Clinton's candidacy and hurt President Trump's. Vogel wrote:

> Ukrainian government officials tried to help Hillary Clinton and undermine Trump by publicly questioning his fitness for office. They also disseminated documents implicating a top Trump aide in corruption and suggested they were investigating the matter, only to back away after the election. And they helped Clinton's allies research damaging information on Trump and his advisers, a *Politico* investigation found.[536]

Vogel reported how Alexandra Chalupa, a Ukrainian-American contractor paid by the DNC and working with the DNC and the Clinton campaign, "traded information and leads" about Paul Manafort, Trump's campaign manager, with staff at the Ukrainian embassy.[537] Chalupa also told Vogel that the Ukrainian embassy "worked directly with reporters researching Trump, Manafort, and Russia to point them in the right directions."[538] With the DNC's encouragement, Chalupa asked Ukrainian embassy staff "to try to arrange an interview in which [Ukrainian President] Poroshenko might discuss Manafort's ties to [Russia-aligned former Ukrainian President Viktor] Yanukovych."[539]

Vogel also spoke on the record to Andrii Telizhenko, a political officer in the Ukrainian Embassy under Ambassador Chaly, who corroborated Chalupa's account.[540] Telizhenko said that he was instructed by Ambassador Chaly's top aide, Oksana Shulyar, to "help Chalupa research connections between Trump, Manafort, and Russia" with the goal of generating a hearing in Congress.[541] Telizhenko also told Vogel that he was instructed not to speak to the Trump campaign:

> We had an order not to talk to the Trump team, because he was critical of Ukraine and the government and his critical position on Crimea and the conflict. I was yelled at when I proposed to talk to Trump. The ambassador said not to get involved – Hillary is going to win.[542]

---

[536] *Id.*

[537] *Id.* In April 2019, then-Ambassador Chaly issued a statement to *The Hill* denying that the Ukrainian embassy sought to influence the election. *See Official April 25, 2019 statement of the Ukrainian embassy in Washington to The Hill concerning the activities of Democratic National Committee Alexandra Chalupa during the 2016 U.S. election*, https://www.scribd.com/document/432699412/Ukraine-Chaly-Statement-on-Chalupa-042519.

[538] Vogel & Stern, *supra* note 127.

[539] *Id.* Interestingly, in August 2019, when Chairman Schiff tweeted an allegation that U.S. security assistance to Ukraine was tied up with Ukrainian investigations, Alexandra Chalupa replied that she had "a lot of information on this topic." *See* Adam Schiff (@RepAdamSchiff), Twitter (Aug. 28, 2019, 5:17 p.m.), https://twitter.com/RepAdamSchiff/status/1166867471862829056. It is unknown whether Chalupa ever provided information to Chairman Schiff or his staff.

[540] Vogel & Stern, *supra* note 127.

[541] *Id.*

[542] *Id.*

Vogel also reported on the actions of Ukrainian parliamentarian Leshchenko, who spoke out against Manafort, in part, to show that candidate Trump was a "pro-Russia candidate."[543] A separate congressional investigation in 2018 learned that Leshchenko was a source for Fusion GPS, the opposition research firm hired by the DNC's law firm, Perkins Coie, to gather information about candidate Trump.[544] Fusion GPS received information about Manafort that may have originated from Leshchenko.[545]

The Democrats' witnesses in the impeachment inquiry testified that the allegations of Ukrainian influence in the 2016 election were appropriate to examine.[546] Asked about the *Politico* reporting, Ambassador Taylor said that, if true, it is "disappointing" that some Ukrainian officials worked against President Trump. He testified:

> Q. So isn't it possible that Trump administration officials might have a good-founded belief, whether true or untrue, that there were forces in the Ukraine that were operating against them?
>
> A. [B]ased on this [January 2017] *Politico* article, which, again, surprises me, disappoints me because I think it's a mistake for any diplomat or any government official in one country to interfere in the political life of another country. That's disappointing.[547]

Ambassador Taylor testified that he was "surprise[d] [and] disappoint[ed]" that Avakov, an influential member of the Ukrainian government—who still serves in President Zelensky's government—had criticized President Trump during the 2016 campaign.[548] He testified:

> Q. What do you know about Avakov?
>
> A. So he is the Minister of Internal Affairs and was the Minister of Internal Affairs under President Poroshenko as one of only two carryovers from the Poroshenko Cabinet to the Zelensky Cabinet. He, as I think I mentioned earlier when we were talking about Lutsenko, the Minister of Interior, which Avakov is now, controls the police, which gives him significant influence in the government.
>
> Q. Avakov, he's a relatively influential Minister. Is that right?
>
> A. That is correct.

---

[543] *Id.*; Olearchyk, *supra* note 123.

[544] Transcribed Interview of Nellie Ohr, in Wash., D.C., at 113-15 (Oct. 19, 2018).

[545] *Id.*

[546] *See, e.g.,* Volker transcribed interview, *supra* note 60, at 146.

[547] Taylor deposition, *supra* note 47, at 101.

[548] *Id.* at 98-99.

Q. Does it concern you that at one time he was being highly critical of candidate Trump?

A. It does.

Q. And did you ever have any awareness of that before I called your attention to this?

A. I haven't. This is surprising. Disappointing, but—[549]

Despite this testimony, Chairman Schiff has prevented Republican Members from fully assessing the nature and extent of Ukraine's influence in the 2016 election. Chairman Schiff refused to invite Alexandra Chalupa or Fusion GPS contractor Nellie Ohr to testify during public hearings.[550] Chairman Schiff declined to concur with a Republican subpoena for documents relating to the DNC's communications with the Ukrainian government.[551] Chairman Schiff declined to concur with a Republican subpoena for documents relating to the DNC's work with Alexandra Chalupa.[552]

* * *

There are legitimate concerns about Burisma's corruption and Hunter Biden's role on the company's board, and Ukrainian government officials' actions to support Secretary Clinton over President Trump in the 2016 election. Democrats reflexively dismiss these concerns because acknowledging them would require an admission that past U.S. assistance to Ukraine may have been misspent. As Ambassador Yovanovitch testified:

> I think most Americans believe that there shouldn't be meddling in our elections. And if Ukraine is the one that had been meddling in our elections, I think the support that all of you [in Congress] have provided to Ukraine over the last almost 30 years, I don't know that – I think people would ask themselves questions about that.[553]

Similarly, other career foreign service employees spoke about their emotional investment in U.S. foreign assistance to Ukraine. Speaking about his reaction to the recent events in Ukraine, Ambassador Taylor testified that he feels a strong "emotional attachment, bond, connection to this country and these people."[554] Deputy Assistant Secretary Kent, according to current State Department employee and former NSC staffer Catherine Croft, likewise "has a lot of emotion tied into" U.S. policy toward Ukraine, saying he "feels very strongly in all aspects of our policy

---

[549] *Id.*

[550] *See, e.g.*, Riley Beggin, *House Democrats deny Republicans' request for whistleblower testimony.* Vox, Nov. 10, 2019.

[551] *Impeachment Inquiry: Ms. Laura Cooper and Mr. David Hale, supra* note 246.

[552] *Id.*

[553] Yovanovitch deposition, *supra* note 115, at 137.

[554] Taylor deposition, *supra* note 47, at 273.

with regard to Ukraine."[555] President Trump's world view threatens these personal, subjective interests, which may explain why some are so eager to discount these allegations.

F. The anonymous whistleblower who served as the basis for the impeachment inquiry has no firsthand knowledge of events and a bias against President Trump.

Democrats built their impeachment inquiry on the foundation of the anonymous whistleblower complaint submitted to the Inspector General of the Intelligence Community on August 12. This foundation is fundamentally flawed.

The anonymous whistleblower acknowledged having no firsthand knowledge about the events he or she described. As a result, his or her complaint mischaracterized important facts and portrayed events in an inaccurate light. The anonymous whistleblower reportedly had a professional relationship with Vice President Joe Biden, which, if true, biases the whistleblower's impressions of the events as they relate to Vice President Biden. The anonymous whistleblower also reportedly communicated initially with House Intelligence Committee Chairman Adam Schiff, who has been an ardent and outspoken critic of President Trump, or his staff. Chairman Schiff's early secret awareness of the issue tainted the objectivity of the Democrats' impeachment inquiry.

To this day, only one Member of Congress—Chairman Schiff—knows the identity of the individual whose words sparked the impeachment of the President. Chairman Schiff has prevented any objective assessment of the whistleblower's credibility or knowledge. Chairman Schiff declined to invite the whistleblower to testify as part of the Democrats' impeachment inquiry, but only after Chairman Schiff's or his staff's communications with the whistleblower came to light.[556] Chairman Schiff rejected a Republican subpoena for documents relating to the drafting of the whistleblower complaint and the whistleblower's personal memorandum written shortly after the July 25 telephone conversation.[557]

The public reporting about the existence of a whistleblower and his or her sensational allegations about President Trump generated tremendous public interest. But Americans cannot assess the credibility, motivations, or biases of the whistleblower. This analysis is necessary because the whistleblower's inaccurate assertions, coupled with Chairman Schiff's selective leaks of cherry-picked information, have prejudiced the public narrative surrounding President Trump's telephone call with President Zelensky.

1. The anonymous whistleblower acknowledged having no firsthand knowledge of the events in question.

The anonymous whistleblower has no direct, firsthand knowledge of the events described in his or her complaint. In the complaint, the whistleblower acknowledged, "I was not a direct

[555] Croft deposition, *supra* note 60, at 105-06.
[556] *See, e.g.*, Beggin, *supra* note 550.
[557] *Impeachment Inquiry: Ms. Laura Cooper and Mr. David Hale, supra* note 246.

witness to most of the events described," and admitted that he or she was not on the July 25 call between President Trump and President Zelensky.[558] Instead, the anonymous whistleblower relied upon indirect, secondhand information provided by others—individuals who are also still unidentified. The whistleblower's lack of firsthand knowledge undermines the credibility of his or her accusations.

Testimony provided by officials with firsthand knowledge of the events rebuts the whistleblower's allegations. Ambassador Sondland testified that some of the concerns in the August 12 whistleblower complaint may be inaccurate or hyperbole.[559] For example, both Ambassador Volker and Ambassador Sondland testified that the whistleblower incorrectly alleged "that State Department officials, including Ambassadors Volker and Sondland, had spoken with Mr. Giuliani to 'contain the damage' to U.S. national security."[560] The ambassadors also disagreed with the whistleblower's statement that they helped Ukrainian leadership "'navigate' the demands" from President Trump.[561]

In addition, Ambassador Sondland took issue with the whistleblower's characterization of efforts to arrange a meeting between President Trump and President Zelensky. The whistleblower complaint stated:

> During this same timeframe, multiple U.S. officials told me [the anonymous whistleblower] that the Ukrainian leadership was led to believe that a meeting or phone call between the President and President Zelensky would depend on whether Zelensky showed willingness to "play ball" on the issues that had been publicly aired by Mr. Lutsenko and Mr. Giuliani.[562]

Ambassador Sondland testified that he never heard U.S. officials use the expression "play ball" in this context.[563]

2. Press reports suggest that the anonymous whistleblower acknowledged having a professional relationship with former Vice President Biden.

The anonymous whistleblower reportedly acknowledged having a professional relationship with Vice President Biden. This admission is important because Vice President Biden was referenced in passing on the July 25 call and is a potential opponent of President Trump in the 2020 presidential election. It stands to reason that a mention of Vice President Biden—no matter how brief or innocuous—could stir the passion of someone who had a professional relationship with him.

---

[558] Whistleblower letter, *supra* note 85, at 1; *see also* Letter from Hon. Michael Atkinson, Inspector Gen. of the Intelligence Cmty., to Hon. Joseph Maguire, Acting Dir. Of Nat'l Intelligence (Aug. 26, 2019).
[559] Sondland deposition, *supra* note 51, at 259-64, 311-14.
[560] Volker transcribed interview, *supra* note 60, at 100-01; Sondland deposition, *supra* note 51, at 261-62, 313.
[561] Volker transcribed interview, *supra* note 60, at 101; Sondland deposition, *supra* note 51, at 259-61, 311-12.
[562] Whistleblower letter, *supra* note 85, at 7.
[563] Sondland deposition, *supra* note 51, at 264.

On August 26, 2019, Inspector General Atkinson wrote to Acting Director of National Intelligence (DNI) Joseph Maguire stating that he found "some indicia of an arguable political bias on the part of the [anonymous whistleblower] in favor of a rival political candidate . . . ."[564] News reports later reported that the "rival political candidate" referenced in Atkinson's letter was a 2020 Democrat presidential candidate with whom that the whistleblower acknowledged having a "professional relationship."[565]

Subsequent news reports explained that the whistleblower is a CIA analyst who had been detailed to the NSC and would have worked closely with Vice President Biden's office.[566] This relationship is significant because President Obama relied upon Vice President Biden to be the Obama Administration's point person for Ukrainian policy.[567] This relationship suggests that aside from any partisan bias in support of Vice President Biden's 2020 presidential campaign, the whistleblower may also have had a bias in favor of Vice President Biden's Ukrainian policies instead of those of President Trump.

3. The anonymous whistleblower secretly communicated with Chairman Schiff or his staff.

According to an admission from Chairman Schiff, the anonymous whistleblower communicated with Chairman Schiff's staff prior to submitting his or her complaint. This early, secret involvement of Chairman Schiff severely prejudices the objectivity of the whistleblower's allegations, given Chairman Schiff's obsession with attacking President Trump for partisan gain.

Since 2016, Chairman Schiff has been a chief ringleader in Congress for asserting that President Trump colluded with Russia, going so far as to allege that he had secret evidence of collusion.[568] Now Chairman Schiff is the investigator-in-chief of President Trump's July 25 phone call with Ukrainian President Zelensky. Chairman Schiff led the investigation's first phase from behind the closed doors of his Capitol basement bunker, even though the depositions were all unclassified. Chairman Schiff did so purely for information control—allowing him to leak selected pieces of information to paint a misleading public narrative.

Chairman Schiff has publicly fabricated evidence about President Trump's July 25 phone call and misled the American public about his awareness of the whistleblower allegations. On September 26, at a public hearing of the House Intelligence Committee, Chairman Schiff opened the proceedings by fabricating the contents of President Trump's call with President Zelensky to

---

[564] Letter from Hon. Michael Atkinson, Inspector General of the Intelligence Community, to Hon. Joseph Maguire, Dir. Of Nat'l Intelligence, Office of the Dir. of Nat'l Intelligence (Aug. 26, 2019).

[565] Byron York, *Whistleblower Had 'Professional' Tie to 2020 Democratic Candidate,* Wash. Exam., Oct. 8, 2019.

[566] *See generally* Rob Crilly, Steven Nelson, & David Drucker, *Joe Biden Worked with Whistleblower When he was Vice President, Officials Reveal,* Wash. Exam., Oct. 10, 2019; Ben Feuerherd, *Whistleblower May Have Worked with Joe Biden in White House: Report,* N.Y. Post, Oct. 10, 2019; Julian Barnes, Michael Schmidt, Adam Goldman, & Katie Benner, *White House Knew of Whistleblower's Allegations Soon After Trump's Call with Ukraine Leader,* N.Y. Times, Sept. 26, 2019.

[567] Greg Myre, *What Were the Bidens Doing in Ukraine? 5 Questions Answered,* Nat'l Pub. Radio, Sept. 24, 2019.

[568] *See, e.g.*, Kelsey Tamborrino, *Warner: 'Enormous amounts of evidence' of possible Russia collusion*, Politico, Mar. 3, 2019.

make the conversation seem sinister.[569] Pretending to be President Trump, Chairman Schiff said in part:

> I hear what you want. I have a favor I want from you though. And I'm going to say this only seven times so you better listen good. I want you to make up dirt on my political opponent, understand. Lots of it.[570]

These words were never uttered by President Trump. When Chairman Schiff rightly faced criticism for his actions, he blamed others for not understanding that he was joking.[571] Republicans sought to hold Chairman Schiff accountable for his fabrication of evidence; however, Democrats prevented the House from voting on a censure resolution.[572]

In October 2019, the *New York Times* reported that the whistleblower contacted a staff member on the House Intelligence Committee—chaired by Chairman Schiff—after asking a colleague to convey his or her concerns about the July 25 call to the CIA's top lawyer.[573] Chairman Schiff, however, had denied ever communicating directly with the whistleblower,[574] and the whistleblower failed to disclose that he or she had contacted Chairman Schiff's staff when asked by the Intelligence Community Inspector General.[575] Chairman Schiff acknowledged his early awareness of the whistleblower's allegations only after he was caught.[576] The *Washington Post* gave Chairman Schiff "Four Pinocchios"—its worst rating—for "clearly ma[king] a statement that was false."[577]

Chairman Schiff's early awareness of the whistleblower complaint explains why he publicly posited a connection between paused U.S. security assistance and Ukrainian investigations well before the whistleblower complaint became public. On August 28, 2019, before the public became aware of the whistleblower complaint or any allegations that U.S. security assistance to Ukraine was linked to Ukraine investigating President Trump's political rival, Chairman Schiff made such a connection in a tweet.[578] According to the *New York Times*, Chairman Schiff knew "the outlines" of the anonymous whistleblower complaint at the time that he issued this tweet.[579]

[569] *Whistleblower disclosure, supra* note 1.
[570] *Id.*
[571] *Id.*
[572] Katherine Tully-McManus, *Republican effort to censure Adam Schiff halted*, Roll Call, Oct. 21, 2019.
[573] Julian Barnes, Michael Schmidt, & Matthew Rosenberg, *Schiff Got Early Account of Accusations as Whistleblower's Concerns Grew*, N.Y. Times, Oct. 2, 2019.
[574] *See, e.g.*, Glenn Kessler, *Schiff's false claim his committee had not spoken to the whistleblower*, Wash. Post, Oct. 4, 2019.
[575] Andrew O'Reilly, *Schiff Admits He Should Have Been 'Much More Clear' About Contact with Whistleblower*, Fox News, Oct. 13, 2019.
[576] *Schiff Got Early Account of Accusations as Whistleblower's Concerns Grew, supra* note 573.
[577] *Schiff's false claim his committee had not spoken to the whistleblower, supra* note 574.
[578] Adam Schiff (@RepAdamSchiff), Twitter, (Aug. 28, 2019, 8:17 PM), https://twitter.com/RepAdamSchiff/status/1166867471862829056.
[579] Barnes, Schmidt, & Rosenberg, *supra* note 573.

Figure 3: Chairman Schiff's August 28 tweet linking aid to investigations

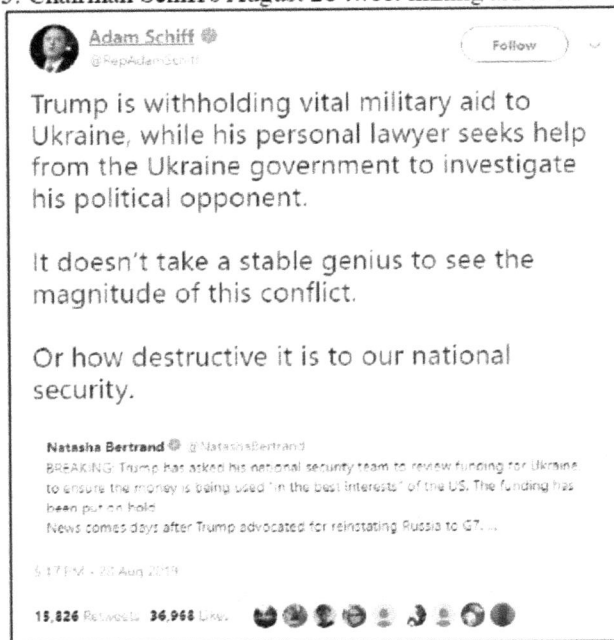

Chairman Schiff's early awareness also explains why he pressured Inspector General Atkinson to produce the whistleblower's complaint to Congress, despite Acting DNI Maguire's determination that transmittal was not required because the complaint did not meet the legal definition of "urgent concern."[580]

* * *

The allegations of the anonymous whistleblower—the foundation for the Democrats' impeachment inquiry—are fundamentally flawed. The whistleblower acknowledged having no direct, firsthand knowledge of the events he or she described. The whistleblower reportedly acknowledged a professional relationship with Vice President Joe Biden, which, if true, suggests a bias toward Vice President Biden and against President Trump. Finally, the whistleblower secretly communicated with staff of Chairman Schiff, who subsequently misled the public about this communication.

If Democrats are serious about impeaching the President—about undoing the will of the American people—they cannot limit the evidence and information available to the House of Representatives. The motivations, biases, and credibility of the anonymous whistleblower are necessary aspects of any serious examination of the facts in question.

---

[580] U.S. Dep't of Justice, Office of Legal Counsel, "Urgent Concern" Determination by the Inspector General of the Intelligence Community 2 (2019).

II. The evidence does not establish that President Trump engaged in a cover-up of his interactions with Ukrainian President Zelensky.

Democrats also argue that President Trump is engaged in a cover-up of his July 25 telephone conversation by hiding evidence of his alleged wrongdoing.[581] There is no basis for this allegation. The President has been transparent about the issues surrounding the anonymous whistleblower complaint and the telephone call with President Zelensky.

On September 24, Speaker Pelosi launched the impeachment inquiry based solely on reports of the telephone call between President Trump and President Zelensky. She had not listened to the conversation; she had not read the call summary or the whistleblower complaint. The following day, to offer unprecedented transparency and prove there was no *quid pro quo*, President Trump declassified the July 25 call summary for the American people to read for themselves. President Trump also released a redacted version of the anonymous whistleblower complaint and he released the summary of his April 21 telephone conversation with President Zelensky. Even the Democrats' best evidence of a "cover-up"—the restricted access to the call summary—is unpersuasive. Evidence suggests that the call summary was restricted not for a malicious intention but as a result of the proliferation of leaks by unelected bureaucrats, including leaks of President Trump's conversations with foreign leaders.

A. President Trump declassified and released publicly the summary of his July 25 phone call with President Zelensky.

On July 25, President Trump and President Zelensky spoke by telephone.[582] Normally, presidential conversations with foreign leaders are presumptively classified because "[t]he unauthorized disclosure of foreign government information is presumed to cause damage to the national security."[583] In fact, the call summary of President Trump's call with President Zelensky was initially marked as classified.[584]

On September 25, after questions arose about the contents of the phone call, President Trump chose to declassify and release the transcript in the interest of full transparency. He wrote on Twitter: "I am currently at the United Nations representing our Country, but have authorized the release tomorrow of the complete, fully declassified and unredacted transcript of my phone conversation with President Zelensky of Ukraine."[585] The President stressed his goal that Americans could read for themselves the contents of the call: "You will see it was a very friendly and totally appropriate call. No pressure unlike Joe Biden and his son, NO quid pro quo! This is

---

[581] *See, e.g.*, Speaker Nancy Pelosi, Transcript of Pelosi Weekly Press Conference (Sept. 26, 2019) ("The [whistleblower] complaint reports 'repeated abuse of an electronics record system designed to store classified, sensitive national security information, which the White House used to hide information of a political nature.' This is a cover-up. This is a cover-up.").

[582] Memorandum of Telephone Conversation, *supra* note 15.

[583] Exec. Order 13,526 (2009).

[584] *See* Memorandum of Telephone Conversation, *supra* note 15.

[585] Donald J. Trump (@realDonaldTrump), Twitter (Sept. 24, 2019, 11:12 a m.), https://twitter.com/realdonaldtrump/status/1176559966024556544.

nothing more than a continuation of the Greatest and most Destructive Witch Hunt of all time."[586]

B. President Trump released a redacted version of the classified anonymous whistleblower complaint.

Like the call summary, the anonymous whistleblower complaint was initially classified. The complaint was reportedly "hand delivered . . . to Capitol Hill" hours after President Trump released the call summary.[587] Although a limited number of Members of Congress—like Chairman Schiff—could access the classified complaint, the American public could not. The President released a redacted version of the anonymous whistleblower complaint so that every American could read it for themselves.[588]

C. President Trump released publicly the summary of his April 21 phone call with President Zelensky.

President Trump first spoke by telephone with President Zelensky on April 21, 2019, the date on which President Zelensky won the Ukrainian presidential election.[589] On November 15, the President publicly released the summary of this April conversation.[590] President Trump explained that he chose to release the summary of this call to "continue being the most transparent President in history."[591]

D. The Trump Administration has experienced a surge in sensitive leaks, including details of the President's communications with foreign leaders.

The Trump Administration has experienced an unprecedented number of potentially damaging leaks from the U.S. national security apparatus.[592] According to a report from the Senate Homeland Security and Governmental Affairs Committee in May 2017, these leaks have flowed seven times faster under President Trump than during former Presidents Obama and Bush's administrations—averaging almost one per day.[593] The report explained:

[586] Donald J. Trump (@realDonaldTrump), Twitter (Sept. 24, 2019, 11:12 a m.), https://twitter.com/realdonaldtrump/status/1176559970390806530.

[587] Dana Bash, et al, *Whistleblower complaint about Trump declassified and may be released Thursday*, CNN, Sept. 26, 2019.

[588] *Whistleblower complaint says White House tried to "lock down" Ukraine call records*, CBS News, Sept. 26, 2019.

[589] *Memorandum of Telephone Conversation, supra* note 10.

[590] Mark Mazzetti & Eileen Sullivan, *Rough transcript of Trump's first phone call with Ukrainian leader released*, N.Y. Times, Nov. 15, 2019.

[591] Donald J. Trump (@realDonaldTrump), Twitter (Nov. 11, 2019, 3:35 p.m.), https://twitter.com/realDonaldTrump/status/1194035922066714625.

[592] HSGAC report, *supra* note 409.

[593] *Id.*

From the morning of President Trump's inauguration, when major newspapers published information about highly sensitive intelligence intercepts, news organizations have reported on an avalanche of leaks from officials across the U.S. government. Many disclosures have concerned the investigations of alleged Russian interference in the 2016 election, with the world learning details of whose communications U.S. intelligence agencies are monitoring, what channels are being monitored, and the results of those intercepts. All such revelations are potential violations of federal law, punishable by jail time.

But the leak frenzy has gone far beyond the Kremlin and has extended to other sensitive information that could harm national security. President Trump's private conversations with other foreign leaders have shown up in the press, while secret operations targeting America's most deadly adversaries were exposed in detail.

As *The New York Times* wrote in a candid self-assessment: "Journalism in the Trump era has featured a staggering number of leaks from sources across the federal government." No less an authority than President Obama's CIA director called the deluge of state secrets "appalling." These leaks do not occur in a vacuum. They can, and do, have real world consequences for national security.[594]

As the *Washington Post* explained, "Every presidential administration leaks. So far, the Trump White House has gushed."[595] Sensitive national security information—for which public disclosure could harm U.S. interests—found its way into mainstream news outlets such as the *New York Times*, the *Washington Post*, NBC, and *Associated Press*.[596] This unfortunate reality helps to explain the circumstances by which the NSC handled the summary of President Trump's July 25 telephone conversation with President Zelensky.

E. The evidence does not establish that access to the July 25 call summary was restricted for inappropriate reasons.

The anonymous whistleblower complaint alleged that NSC staffers deliberately placed the call summary of the July 25 call on a highly secure server to hide its contents.[597] This allegation has not been proven. In fact, the Democrats' witnesses testified that it was mistakenly place on a highly classified server. Evidence suggests that call summaries of the President's conversations with other foreign leaders have been subject to restricted access due to a pattern of leaks.

---

[594] *Id.*

[595] Paul Farhi, *The Trump administration has sprung a leak. Many of them, in fact*, Wash. Post, Feb. 5, 2017.

[596] HSGAC report, *supra* note 409.

[597] Whistleblower letter, *supra* note 85.

As the Trump Administration dealt with an unprecedented number of national security leaks, it sought to take appropriate precautions. Public reporting indicates that the NSC began restricting access to summaries of the President's communications with foreign leaders following the leak of President Trump's conversation in May 2017 with senior Russian officials.[598] Dr. Fiona Hill, the former NSC Senior Director for Europe, testified that a summary of this meeting was not initially restricted and that details of the conversation "seemed to immediately end up in the press."[599] Following this leak, the White House began a practice of restricting access to summaries of calls and meetings with foreign leaders.[600] Current and former White House officials said that it made sense to restrict access to calls given the number of leaks.[601]

With respect to the summary of President Trump's conversation with President Zelensky on July 25, NSC Senior Director Tim Morrison testified in his closed-door deposition that although he "was not concerned that anything illegal was discussed," he was concerned about a leak of the summary of President Trump's call with President Zelensky.[602] He explained that he was "concerned about how the contents [of the call summary] would be used in Washington's political process."[603] In his public testimony, Morrison elaborated:

> Q. And you were concerned about it leaking because you were worried about how it would play out in Washington's polarized political environment, correct?
>
> A. Yes.
>
> Q. And you were also worried how that would lead to the bipartisan support here in Congress towards Ukraine, right?
>
> A. Yes.
>
> Q. And you were also concerned that it might affect the Ukrainians' perception negatively.
>
> A. Yes.
>
> Q. And, in fact, all three of those things have played out, haven't they?
>
> A. Yes.[604]

---

[598] *See, e.g.*, Julian E. Barnes et al., *White House Classified Computer System is Used to Hold Transcripts of Sensitive Calls*, N.Y. Times, Sept. 29, 2019.

[599] Hill deposition, *supra* note 12, at 294.

[600] Barnes, et al., *supra* note 598.

[601] *Id.*

[602] Morrison deposition, *supra* note 12, at 16.

[603] *Id.* at 44.

[604] *Impeachment Inquiry: Ambassador Kurt Volker and Timothy Morrison, supra* note 8.

LTC Vindman—the NSC staffer who raised concerns about the contents of call—testified there was no "malicious intent" in restricting access to the summary.[605] Morrison also testified that call summary was mistakenly placed on a secure server with restricted access.[606] He explained:

> Q. And were you ever provided with an explanation for why [the call summary] was placed in the highly classified system?
>
> A. Yes.
>
> Q. What was the explanation you were given?
>
> A. It was a mistake.
>
> Q. It was a mistake?
>
> A. Yes.[607]

In his public testimony, Morrison reiterated that the placement of the call summary on a secure server was an administrative error.[608] He explained that NSC Legal Advisor John Eisenberg sought to restrict access to the summary, but that his direction was mistakenly interpreted to mean placing the summary on a secure server.[609] He testified:

> I spoke with the NSC Executive Secretariat staff, asked them why [the summary had been removed from the normal server]. And they did their research, and they informed me it had been moved to the higher classification system at the direction of John Eisenberg, whom I then asked why. I mean, that's – if that was the judgment he made, that's not necessarily mine to question, but I didn't understand it. And he essentially told me, "I gave no such direction." He did his own inquiry, and he represented back to me that it was – his understanding was that it was a kind of administrative error, that when he also gave direction to restrict access, the Executive Secretariat staff understood that as an apprehension that there was something in the content of the [call summary] that could not exist on the lower classification system.[610]

Morrison also explained that there was no malicious intent in moving the transcript to the secure server.[611]

---

[605] Vindman deposition, *supra* note 12, at 124.
[606] Morrison deposition, *supra* note 12, at 54-57.
[607] *Id.* at 54.
[608] *Impeachment Inquiry: Ambassador Kurt Volker and Timothy Morrison, supra* note 8.
[609] *Id.*
[610] *Id.*
[611] *Id.*

To the extent Democrats allege that President Trump sought to cover up his July 25 telephone conversation with President Zelensky, the facts do not support such a charge. Indeed, President Trump has declassified and publicly released the July 25 call summary. He has also released a redacted version of the classified anonymous whistleblower complaint and released the call summary of his first phone call with President Zelensky, on April 21. Although the July 25 call summary was located on a secure White House server prior to its public release, testimony shows that its placement on the server was an "administrative error." In light of substantial leaks of sensitive national security information—including the President's conversations with foreign leaders—testimony shows that the NSC Legal Advisor sought to restrict access to the summary. In attempting to carry out this direction, the NSC executive secretariat staff incorrectly placed the summary on a secure server. Taken, together, these facts do not establish that President Trump sought to cover up his interactions with President Zelensky.

III. The evidence does not establish that President Trump obstructed Congress in the Democrats' impeachment inquiry.

Democrats allege that President Trump has obstructed Congress by declining to participate in Speaker Pelosi's impeachment inquiry.[612] Under any fair assessment of the facts, however, President Trump has not obstructed Congress. In fact, the President personally urged at least one witness to cooperate with the Democrats' impeachment inquiry and to testify truthfully.[613] But Democrats cannot and should not impeach President Trump for declining to submit himself to an abusive and unfair process.

In the Democrats' impeachment inquiry, fairness is not an asset guaranteed or even recognized. Democrats have told witnesses in the inquiry that a failure to adhere strictly to their demands "shall constitute evidence of obstruction of the House's impeachment inquiry and may be used as an adverse inference against the President."[614] Democrats have threatened to withhold the salaries for agency employees as punishment for not meeting Democrat demands.[615] As Chairman Schiff explained the Democrat logic, any disagreement with Democrats amounts to obstruction: "The failure to produce this witness, the failure to produce these documents, we consider yet additionally strong evidence of obstruction of the constitutional functions of Congress, a coequal branch of government."[616]

The Democrats' actions are fundamentally abusive. In any just proceeding, the President ought to be afforded an opportunity to raise defenses without Democrats considering it to be *de facto* evidence of obstruction. In any just proceeding, investigators would not impute the conduct of a witness to the President or use a witness's refusal to cooperate with an unfair process as an "adverse inference" against the President.

The Democrats' obstruction arguments are also divorced from historical precedent for House impeachment proceedings and basic legal concepts of due process and the presumption of innocence. Past bipartisan precedent for presidential impeachment inquiries guaranteed fundamental fairness by authorizing bipartisan subpoena authority; providing the President unrestricted access to information presented; and allowing the President's counsel to identify relevant witnesses and evidence, cross examine witnesses, and respond to evidence collected. These guarantees of due process and fundamental fairness are not present in the Democrats' impeachment resolution against President Trump.

Congressional oversight of the Executive Branch is an important and serious undertaking designed to improve the efficiency and accountability of the federal government. The White House has said that it is willing to work with Democrats on legitimate congressional oversight

---

[612] *See, e.g.*, Amber Phillips, *How the House Could Impeach Trump for Obstructing its Probe*, Wash. Post, Oct. 8, 2019.

[613] Sondland deposition, *supra* note 51, at 38.

[614] *See, e.g.*, letter from Eliot L. Engel, Chairman, H. Comm. on Foreign Affairs, et al. to John Eisenberg, Nat'l Sec. Council (Oct. 30, 2019).

[615] *See* letter from Eliot L. Engel, Chairman, H. Comm. on Foreign Affairs, et al. to John J. Sullivan, Dep. Sec'y, Dep't of State (Oct. 1, 2019).

[616] Phillips, *supra* note 612.

requests.[617] However, public statements from prominent Democrats suggest they are pursuing impeachment purely for partisan reasons—that they seeking to prevent President Trump's reelection in 2020.[618] The Democrats' unfair and abusive impeachment process confirms that they are not interested in pursuing a full understanding of the facts.

Even despite the Democrats' partisan rhetoric and unfair process, President Trump has been transparent about his interactions with Ukrainian President Zelensky. President Trump has released to the public documents directly relevant the subject matter and he has spoken publicly about the issues. Democrats cannot justly condemn President Trump for declining to submit to their abusive and fundamentally unfair process.

A. Democrats have abandoned long-standing precedent by failing to guarantee due process and fundamental fairness in their impeachment inquiry.

The two recent impeachment investigations into presidents by the House of Representatives were largely identical to each other despite the passage of two decades. In 1974, the House authorized an impeachment inquiry into President Nixon by debating and passing House Resolution 803.[619] This resolution authorized the Committee on the Judiciary to issue subpoenas, including those offered by the minority; to sit and act without regard to whether the House stood in recess; and to expend funds in the pursuit of the investigation.[620] In 1998, the House passed House Resolution 581, a nearly identical resolution authorizing an impeachment inquiry into President Clinton.[621]

In 1974, the House undertook this action because "the rule of the House defining the jurisdiction of committees does not place jurisdiction over impeachment matters in the Judiciary Committee. In fact, it does not place such jurisdiction anywhere."[622] Passing a resolution authorizing the inquiry was "a necessary step if we are to meet our obligations [under the Constitution]."[623] By passing the resolution, the House sought to make "[t]he committee's investigative authority . . . fully coextensive with the power of the House in an impeachment investigation . . . ."[624]

Notably, in empowering the Judiciary Committee to conduct the Nixon impeachment inquiry, the House granted subpoena power to the minority, an action that was "against all precedents" at the time.[625] During debate, Members made it "crystal clear that the authority given to the minority [ranking] member and to the chairman, the right to exercise authority [to issue a

---

[617] *See* letter from Pat A. Cipollone, Counsel to the President to Speaker Nancy Pelosi et al. 8 (Oct. 8, 2019).

[618] *See, e.g., Weekends with Alex Witt* (MSNBC television broadcast May 5 2019) (interview with Rep. Al Green).

[619] H. Res. 803, 93rd Cong. (1974).

[620] *See Id.*

[621] H. Res. 581, 105th Cong. (1998).

[622] 130 Cong. Rec. 2351 (Feb. 6, 1974) (statement of Rep. Hutchinson).

[623] *Id.* at 2350 (statement of Rep. Rodino).

[624] H.R. Rep. No. 93-774, at 3 (1974).

[625] 130 Cong. Rec. at 2352 (statement of Rep. Brooks).

subpoena], is essentially the same. It is the same. Both are subject to a veto by a majority of the membership of that committee."[626]

In 1998, the House similarly passed a resolution authorizing an impeachment inquiry because the "[Judiciary] Committee decided that it must receive authorization from the full House before proceeding . . . ."[627] The Judiciary Committee reached this conclusion "[b]ecause impeachment is delegated solely to the House of Representatives by the Constitution, [and therefore] the full House of Representatives should be involved in critical decision making regarding various stages of impeachment."[628]

In putting forth this resolution for consideration by the House, the Judiciary Committee made several commitments with respect to ensuring "procedural fairness" of the impeachment inquiry. For instance, the Judiciary Committee voted to allow the President or his counsel to be present at all executive sessions and open hearings and to allow the President's counsel to cross examine witnesses, make objections regarding relevancy, suggest additional evidence or witnesses that the committee should receive, and to respond to the evidence collected.[629]

The fundamental fairness and due process protections guaranteed in the Nixon and Clinton impeachment proceedings are missing from Speaker Pelosi's impeachment inquiry. The Democrats' impeachment inquiry offers a veneer of legitimacy that hides a deeply partisan and one-sided process. The impeachment resolution passed by Democrats in the House—against bipartisan opposition—allows Democrats to maintain complete control of the proceedings.[630] The resolution denies Republicans co-equal subpoena authority and requires the Democrat chairmen to concur with Republican subpoenas—unlike Democrat subpoenas, which the chairmen may issue with no Republican input.[631] The Democrat impeachment resolution requires Republicans to specifically identify and explain the need for witnesses 72 hours before the first impeachment hearing—without a similar requirement for Democrats.[632] Most importantly, the Democrats' resolution excludes the President's counsel from House Intelligence Committee Chairman Adam Schiff's proceedings and provides House Judiciary Committee Chairman Jerry Nadler with discretion to do the same.[633] In short, these partisan procedures dramatically contradict the bipartisan Nixon and Clinton precedents.

B. Democrats have engaged in an abusive process toward a pre-determined outcome.

Since the beginning of the 116 Congress, Democrats have sought to impeach President Trump. Just hours after her swearing in, Rep. Rashida Tlaib told a crowd at a public event that

---

[626] *Id.*
[627] H.R. Rep. No. 105-795, at 24 (1998).
[628] *Id.*
[629] *Id.* at 25-26.
[630] H. Res. 660, 116th Cong. (2019).
[631] *Id.*
[632] *Id.*
[633] *Id.*

"[Democrats are] going to go in there, and we're going to impeach the [expletive deleted]."[634] Rep. Brad Sherman introduced articles of impeachment against President Trump on the very first day of the Democrat majority.[635] Rep. Al Green separately introduced articles of impeachment in July 2019, and even forced the House to consider the measure.[636] The House tabled Rep. Green's impeachment resolution by an overwhelming bipartisan majority—332 ayes to 95 nays.[637]

Such a fervor to impeach a political opponent for purely partisan reasons was what Alexander Hamilton warned of as the "greatest danger" in Federalist No. 65: that "the decision [to impeach] will be regulated more by the comparative strength of parties, than by the real demonstrations of innocence or guilt."[638] Indicative of this partisan fervor, Democrats have already forced the House to consider three resolutions of impeachment—offered by Democrats after no investigation, report, or process of any kind—since President Trump took office.[639]

During the consideration of articles of impeachment against President Clinton, Democrats argued that "[i]f we are to impeach the President, it should be at the end of a fair process. . . . [and not through decisions] made on a strictly partisan basis."[640] Rep. Zoe Lofgren, now a senior member of the Judiciary Committee, testified then before the Rules Committee on the resolution authorizing the Clinton impeachment inquiry. She said:

> Under our Constitution, the House of Representatives has the sole power of impeachment. This is perhaps our single most serious responsibility short of a declaration of war. Given the gravity and magnitude of this undertaking, only a fair and bipartisan approach to this question will ensure that truth is discovered, honest judgments rendered, and the constitutional requirement observed. Our best yardstick is our historical experience. We must compare the procedures used today with what Congress did a generation ago when a Republican President was investigated by a Democratic House.[641]

However, Speaker Pelosi's impeachment inquiry has been divorced from historical experience and has borne no markings of a fair process. During the first several weeks, the Speaker asserted that a vote authorizing the inquiry was unnecessary.[642] This process allowed Chairman Schiff to conduct his partisan inquiry behind closed doors with only a limited group of Members present. It also allowed Chairman Schiff to selectively leak cherry-picked information

[634] Nicholas Fandos, *Rashida Tlaib's Expletive-Laden Cry to Impeach Trump Upends Democrats' Talking Points*, N.Y. Times, Jan. 4, 2019.

[635] H. Res. 13, 116th Cong. (2019).

[636] H. Res. 498, 116th Cong. (2019).

[637] *Id.* (Roll call vote 483).

[638] Federalist No. 65 (Alexander Hamilton).

[639] *See* H. Res. 646, 115th Cong. (2018); H. Res. 705, 115th Cong. (2018); H. Res. 498, 116th Cong. (2019).

[640] Impeachment Inquiry: William Jefferson Clinton, President of the United States, 105th Cong., Consideration of Articles of Impeachment 82 (Comm. Print 1998) (statement of Rep. Bobby Scott).

[641] *Hearing before the Committee on Rules on H. Res. 525*, 105th Cong., 2d Sess. 108 (1998).

[642] *See, e.g.*, Haley Byrd, *Kevin McCarthy Calls on Nancy Pelosi to Suspend Impeachment Inquiry*, CNN, Oct. 3, 2019.

to paint a misleading public narrative. Chairman Schiff failed to respond to Republican requests for witnesses,[643] and directed witnesses not to answer questions from Republicans.[644] Chairman Schiff even declined to share closed-door deposition transcripts with Republican Members.[645]

During the public hearings, despite the modicum of minority rights outlined in the Democrats' impeachment resolution, Chairman Schiff has continued to trample long-held minority rights. Chairman Schiff interrupted Republican Members during questioning and directed witnesses not to answer Republican questions.[646] Chairman Schiff declined to invite all the witnesses identified by Republicans as relevant to the inquiry.[647] Chairman Schiff declined to honor Republican subpoenas for documents and witnesses, and then violated House rules and the Democrats' impeachment resolution to vote down the subpoenas without sufficient notice or even any debate.[648]

This is the very sort of process that Democrats had previously decried as "what happens when a legislative chamber is obsessively preoccupied with investigating the opposition rather than legislating for the people who elected them to office."[649] Rep. Jerrold Nadler, now chairman of the Judiciary Committee, once argued that:

> The effect of impeachment is to overturn the popular will of voters as expressed in a national election. . . . ***There must never be a narrowly voted impeachment or an impeachment substantially supported by one of our major political parties and largely opposed by the other***. Such an impeachment would lack legitimacy and produce the divisiveness and bitterness in our politics for years to come and will call into question the very legitimacy of our political institutions.[650]

During the impeachment proceedings for President Clinton, Democrats warned against "dump[ing] mountains of salacious, uncross-examined and otherwise untested materials onto the Internet, and then . . . sorting through boxes of documents to selectively find support for a foregone conclusion."[651] But now, in Speaker Pelosi's impeachment inquiry, as conducted by Chairman Schiff, the Democrats' old warnings have become the very process by which their current impeachment inquiry has proceeded.

---

[643] Letter from Jim Jordan, Ranking Member, H. Comm. on Oversight & Reform, et al., to Adam Schiff, Chairman, H. Perm. Sel. Comm. on Intelligence (Oct. 23, 2019).

[644] *See, e.g.*, Vindman deposition, *supra* note 12, at 78-80, 103-05.

[645] *See, e.g.*, Deirdre Shesgreen & Bart Jansen, *House Republicans complain about limited access to closed-door House impeachment investigation sessions*, USA Today, Oct. 16, 2019.

[646] *See, e.g.*, *Impeachment Inquiry: Ambassador William B. Taylor and Mr. George Kent*, *supra* note 2; *Impeachment Inquiry: Ambassador Marie Yovanovitch*, *supra* note 4.

[647] *See, e.g.*, Beggin, *supra* note 550.

[648] *Impeachment Inquiry: Ms. Laura Cooper and Mr. David Hale*, *supra* note 246.

[649] Impeachment Inquiry: William Jefferson Clinton, President of the United States, *supra* note 640, at 94 (statement of Rep. Zoe Lofgren).

[650] *Id.* at 77 (statement of Rep. Jerrold Nadler) (emphasis added).

[651] *Id.* at 82 (statement of Rep. Bobby Scott).

C. President Trump may raise privileges and defenses in response to unfair, abusive proceedings.

Speaker Pelosi's impeachment inquiry, as conducted by Chairman Schiff, has abandoned due process and the presumption of innocence that lies at the heart of western legal systems.[652] Due to this abusive conduct and the Democrats' relentless attacks on the Trump Administration, President Trump may be rightly concerned about receiving fair treatment from House Democrats during this impeachment inquiry.

During the Clinton impeachment proceedings, Rep. Bobby Scott, now a senior member of the Democrat caucus, argued that the impeachment process should "determine[], with a presumption of innocence, whether those allegations [against President Clinton] were true by using cross-examination of witnesses and other traditionally reliable evidentiary procedures."[653] Similarly, Rep. Jerrold Nadler argued then that "[w]e have been entrusted with the grave and awesome duty by the American people, by the Constitution and by history. We must exercise that duty responsibly. At a bare minimum, that means *the President's accusers must go beyond hearsay and innuendo and beyond demands that the President prove his innocence of vague and changing charges*."[654]

Furthermore, Democrats had previously argued that the assertion of privileges by a president does not constitute an impeachable offense. During the Clinton impeachment proceedings, Rep. Scott stated:

> At the hearing when I posed the question of whether any of the witnesses on the hearing's second panel believed that the count involving invoking executive privilege should be considered an impeachable offense, the clear consensus on the panel was that the charge was not an impeachable offense. In fact, one Republican witness said, I do not think invoking executive privilege even if frivolously, and I believe it was frivolous in these circumstances, that that does not constitute an impeachable offense.[655]

Despite this prior commitment to due process and a presumption of innocence, the Democrats now favor a presumption of guilt. Chairman Schiff has said publicly that the Trump Administration and witnesses asserting their constitutional rights and seeking to test the soundness of subpoenas have formed "a very powerful case against the president for obstruction, an article of impeachment based on obstruction."[656] Similarly, Chairman Schiff has made clear

---

[652] *See, e.g., Id.* at 102 (statement of Rep. Maxine Waters) ("As Members of Congress have sworn to uphold the Constitution, we must always insist on equal and just treatment under the law. The presumption of innocence until proven guilty is central and basic to our system of justice.").

[653] *Id.* at 82 (statement of Rep. Bobby Scott).

[654] *Id.* at 78 (statement of Rep. Jerrold Nadler) (emphasis added).

[655] *Id.* at 83 (statement of Rep. Bobby Scott).

[656] Kyle Cheney, *Trump Makes 'Very Powerful Case' for Impeachment Based on Obstruction, Schiff Warns*, Politico, Oct. 28, 2019.

that he will simply assume that a witness's testimony is adverse to the President when that witness or the President asserts a right or privilege.[657] These are not the hallmarks of a fair and transparent process; these are the tell-tale signs of a star chamber.

D. Although declining to submit to the Democrats' abusive and unfair process, President Trump has released information to help the American public understand the issues.

Just twenty-seven minutes after President Trump's inauguration on January 20, 2017, the *Washington Post* reported that the "campaign to impeach President Trump has begun."[658] As the *Post* reported:

> The effort to impeach President Donald John Trump is already underway. At the moment the new commander in chief was sworn in, a campaign to build public support for his impeachment went live at ImpeachDonaldTrumpNow.org, spearheaded by two liberal advocacy groups aiming to lay the groundwork for his eventual ejection from the White House. . . . The impeachment drive comes as Democrats and liberal activists are mounting broad opposition to stymie Trump's agenda.[659]

In 2017 and 2018, Democrats introduced four separation resolution in the House with the goal of impeaching President Trump.[660] On January 3, 2019, on the Democrats' first day in power, Rep. Al Green again introduced articles of impeachment.[661] That same day, Rep. Rashida Tlaib promised, "we're going to go in there and we're going to impeach the [expletive deleted]."[662]

In this context, it is difficult to see the Democrats' impeachment inquiry as anything other than a partisan effort to undo the results of the 2016 election. Rep. Green said on MSNBC in May 2019, "If we don't impeach this President, he will get re-elected."[663] Even as Democrats have conducted their impeachment inquiry, Speaker Pelosi has called President Trump "an impostor" and said it is "dangerous" to allow American voters to evaluate his performance in

---

[657] *See Id.* ("Schiff also argued that the president is seeking to block Kupperman because he is concerned about a high-level source corroborating damning testimony that Trump pressured Ukraine to open investigations of his political rivals—and condition military aid and a White House visit on bending the European ally to his will.").

[658] Matea Gold, *The campaign to impeach President Trump has begun*, Wash. Post, Jan. 20, 2017.

[659] *Id.*

[660] H., Res. 705, 115th Cong. (2018); H. Res. 646, 115th Cong. (2017); H. Res. 621, 115th Cong. (2017); H. Res. 438, 115th Cong. (2017).

[661] H. Res. 13, 116th Cong. (2019).

[662] Amy B. Wong, *Rep. Rashida Tlaib profanely promised to impeach Trump. She's not sorry.*, Wash. Post, Jan. 4, 2019.

[663] *Weekends with Alex Witt, supra* note 618.

2020.[664] The Democrats' impeachment process has mirrored this rhetoric, stacking the deck against the President.[665]

Even so, the President is not entirely unwilling to cooperate with the Democrats' demands. In October 2019, Pat A. Cipollone, the Counsel to the President, wrote to Speaker Pelosi and the chairmen of the three "impeachment" committees:

> If the Committees wish to return to the regular order of oversight requests, we stand ready to engage in that process as we have in the past, in a manner consistent with well-established bipartisan constitutional protections and a respect for the separation of powers enshrined in our Constitution.[666]

Speaker Pelosi did not respond to Mr. Cipollone's letter. President Trump explained that he would "like people to testify" but he is resisting the Democrats' unfair and abusive process "for future Presidents and the Office of the President."[667]

Although the Democrats' abusive and unfair process has prevented his cooperation with the Democrats' impeachment inquiry, President Trump has nonetheless been transparent about his conduct. On September 25, President Trump declassified and released to the public the summary of his July 25 phone conversation with President Zelensky, stressing his goal that Americans could read for themselves the contents of the call: "You will see it was a very friendly and totally appropriate call."[668] On November 15, President Trump released to the public the summary of this April 21 phone conversation with President Zelensky in the interest of transparency.[669] In addition, President Trump has spoken publicly about his actions, as has Acting Chief of Staff Mick Mulvaney.[670]

Congress has a serious and important role to play in overseeing the Executive Branch. When the House of Representatives considers impeachment of a president, bipartisan precedent dictates fundamental fairness and due process. In pursuing impeachment of President Trump, however, Democrats have abandoned those principles, choosing instead to use impeachment as a tool to pursue their partisan objectives. While the President has declined to submit himself to the Democrats' unfair and abusive process, he has still made an effort to be transparent with the Americans to whom he is accountable. Under these abusive and unfair circumstances, the Democrats cannot establish a charge of obstruction.

---

[664] Emily Tillett, *Nancy Pelosi says Trump's attacks on witnesses "very significant" to impeachment probe*, CBS News, Nov. 15, 2019; Dear Colleague Letter from Speaker Nancy Pelosi (Nov. 18, 2019).

[665] *See* H. Res. 660, 116th Cong. (2019).

[666] Letter from Pat A. Cipollone, *supra* note 617.

[667] Donald J. Trump (@realDonaldTrump), Twitter (Nov. 26, 2019, 7:43 a m.), https://twitter.com/realDonaldTrump/status/1199352946187800578.

[668] Donald J. Trump (@realDonaldTrump), Twitter (Sept. 24, 2019, 11:12 a m.), https://twitter.com/realdonaldtrump/status/1176559970390806530.

[669] Donald J. Trump (@realDonaldTrump), Twitter (Nov. 11, 2019, 3:35 p.m.), https://twitter.com/realDonaldTrump/status/1194035922066714625.

[670] *See, e.g.*, The White House, Remarks by President Trump before Marine One Departure (Nov. 20, 2019); Press Briefing by Acting Chief of Staff Mick Mulvaney, *supra* note 302.

IV.   Conclusion

The impeachment of a president is one of the gravest and most solemn duties of the House of Representatives. For Democrats, impeachment is a tool for settling political scores and re-litigating election results with which they disagreed. This impeachment inquiry and the manner in which the Democrats are pursuing it sets a dangerous precedent.

The Democrats have not established an impeachable offense. The evidence presented in this report does not support a finding that President Trump pressured President Zelensky to investigate his political rival for the President's benefit in the 2020 election. The evidence does not establish that President Trump withheld a White House meeting to pressure President Zelensky to investigate his political rival to benefit him in the 2020 election. The evidence does not support that President Trump withheld U.S. security assistance to pressure President Zelensky to investigate his political rival for the President's benefit in the 2020 election. The evidence does not establish that President Trump orchestrated a shadow foreign policy apparatus to pressure President Zelensky to investigate his political rival to benefit him in the 2020 election.

The best evidence of President Trump's interaction with President Zelensky is the "complete and accurate" call summary prepared by the White House Situation Room staff. The summary shows no indication of conditionality, pressure, or coercion. Both President Trump and President Zelensky have denied the existence of any pressure. President Zelensky and his senior advisers in Kyiv did not even know that U.S. security assistance to Ukraine was paused until it was publicly reported in U.S. media. Ultimately, Ukraine received the security assistance and President Zelensky met with President Trump, all without Ukraine ever investigating President Trump's political rival. These facts alone severely undercut the Democrat allegations.

The evidence in the Democrats' impeachment inquiry shows that President Trump is skeptical about U.S. taxpayer-funded foreign assistance and strongly believes that European allies should shoulder more of the financial burden for regional defense. The President also has deeply-rooted, reasonable, and genuine concerns about corruption in Ukraine, including the placement of Vice President Biden's son on the board of a Ukrainian energy company notorious for corruption at a time when Vice President Biden was the Obama Administration's point person for Ukraine policy. There is also compelling and indisputable evidence that Ukrainian government officials—some working with a Democrat operative—sought to influence the U.S. presidential election in 2016 in favor of Secretary Clinton and in opposition to President Trump.

The Democrats' impeachment narrative ignores the President's state of mind and it ignores the specific and concrete actions that the new Zelensky government took to address pervasive Ukrainian corruption. The Democrats' case rests almost entirely on hearsay, presumption, and emotion. Where there are ambiguous facts, the Democrats interpret them in a light most unfavorable to the President. The Democrats also flatly disregard any perception of potential wrongdoing with respect to Hunter Biden's presence on the board of Burisma Holdings or Ukrainian influence in the 2016 election.

The evidence presented also does not support allegations that President Trump covered-up his conversation with President Zelensky by restricting access to it. In light of leaks of other presidential conversations with world leaders, the White House took reasonably steps to restrict access to the July 25 call summary. The summary was mistakenly placed on a secure server; however, the Democrats' witnesses explained that there was no nefarious conduct or malicious intent associated with this action.

Likewise, the evidence presented does not support allegations that President Trump obstructed the Democrats' impeachment inquiry by raising concerns about an unfair and abusive process. The Democrats deviated from prior bipartisan precedent for presidential impeachment and denied Republican attempts to inject basic fairness and objectivity into their partisan and one-sided inquiry. The White House has signaled that it is willing to work with Democrats but President Trump cannot be faulted for declining to submit himself to the Democrats' star chamber. Even so, President Trump has been transparent with the American people about his actions, releasing documents and speaking publicly about the subject matter.

The Democrats' impeachment inquiry paints a picture of unelected bureaucrats within the foreign policy and national security apparatus who fundamentally disagreed with President Trump's style, world view, and decisions. Their disagreements with President Trump's policies and their discomfort with President Trump's actions set in motion the anonymous, secondhand whistleblower complaint. Democrats seized on the whistleblower complaint to fulfill their years-old obsession with removing President Trump from office.

The unfortunate collateral damage of the Democrats' impeachment inquiry is the harm done to bilateral U.S.-Ukraine relations, the fulfillment of Russian President Vladimir Putin's desire to sow discord within the United States, and the opportunity costs to the American people. In the time that Democrats spent investigating the President, Democrats could have passed legislation to implement the U.S.-Mexico-Canada Agreement, lower the costs of prescription drugs, or secure our southern border. Instead, the Democrats' obsession with impeaching President Trump has paralyzed their already-thin legislative agenda. Less than a year before the 2020 election and Democrats in the House still cannot move on from the results of the last election.

www.ingramcontent.com/pod-product-compliance
Lightning Source LLC
Chambersburg PA
CBHW080625030426
42336CB00018B/3081